Courageous
Women of

**Katherine Kenny and
Eleanor Randrup**

4880 Lower Valley Road, Atglen, Pennsylvania 19310

Other Schiffer Books on Related Subjects:

Lord Calvert and the Maryland Adventure, 978-0-7643-3685-0, $9.99
Lost Towns of Tidewater Maryland, 978-0-87033-527-3, $36.95
Annapolis: A Walk Through History, 978-0-87033-546-4, $12.95
The Patapsco: Baltimore's River of History, 978-0-87033-400-9, $22.95

Copyright © 2010 by Katherine Kenny and Eleanor Randrup
Library of Congress Control Number: 2010936426

Designed by "Sue"
Type set in Myriad Pro/Minion Pro

ISBN: 978-0-7643-3541-9
Printed in The United States of America

Schiffer Books are available at special discounts for bulk purchases for sales promotions or premiums. Special editions, including personalized covers, corporate imprints, and excerpts can be created in large quantities for special needs. For more information contact the publisher:

Published by Schiffer Publishing Ltd.
4880 Lower Valley Road
Atglen, PA 19310
Phone: (610) 593-1777; Fax: (610) 593-2002
E-mail: Info@schifferbooks.com

For the largest selection of fine reference books on this and related subjects, please visit our web site at **www.schifferbooks.com**
We are always looking for people to write books on new and related subjects. If you have an idea for a book please contact us at the above address.

This book may be purchased from the publisher. Include $5.00 for shipping.
Please try your bookstore first.
You may write for a free catalog.

In Europe, Schiffer books are distributed by
Bushwood Books
6 Marksbury Ave.
Kew Gardens
Surrey TW9 4JF England
Phone: 44 (0) 20 8392 8585; Fax: 44 (0) 20 8392 9876
E-mail: info@bushwoodbooks.co.uk
Website: www.bushwoodbooks.co.uk

Success is not a gender issue.

-The Authors

Contents

Acknowledgments

We are indebted to many people for helping us with this book. We thank them for giving their time for oral interviews, providing photographs, or aiding with research.

Online Interviews: Leonard Bahr, Elizabeth Fox, Maurice Fox, and Barbara Mikulski.

Oral Interviews: Mary Bahr, Helen Delich Bentley, Lorna Catling, Ada Schrock, Christopher Wilson, John Wilson, Deborah Yow, and Dr. William H. Zinkham

Proofreader: Sue Chapelle

Research: Jeff Korman, Enoch Pratt Free Library; Chris Kintzel, Maryland State Archives, Annapolis, Maryland; Jill Moss Greenberg, Maryland Women's Heritage Center; Linda Shevitz, Maryland Women's Heritage Center; Peggy Nixon, Spruce Forest Artisan Village, Grantsville, Maryland; Barbara O'Brien, Reference Librarian, McDaniel College, Westminster, Maryland; Mary Jo Price, Special Collections Librarian, Frostburg State University; Lori Romero, Director, White Pine County Library, Ely, Nevada; The Frederick Historical Society, Frederick, Maryland; The Maryland Historical Society, Baltimore, Maryland; The Roland Park Country School, Baltimore, Maryland; and Washington County Free Library, Hagerstown, Maryland.

Thank you, Tom and Pete, for your advice and patience. And thank you Pete for graciously chauffeuring us to various destinations throughout Maryland.

Introduction

The inspiration for writing this book came from the authors' many years of teaching at the Roland Park Country School (RPCS) in Baltimore, Maryland. Part of the school's 4th grade curriculum was a unit on courageous women. Over time the teachers looked to include more contemporary figures. There was very little information and nothing available for this age group. And so with retirement, we had time and opportunity to research and write, *Courageous Women of Maryland.*

Not long ago, as we talked with a kindergarten class at RPCS about leadership, one alert 5-year-old said, "I think there's a law you have to be a boy." Maryland has a history of extraordinary women who have made significant contributions to the state and to mankind. Many, such as Rachel Carson and Harriett Tubman, are well known. We wanted to highlight additional individuals who accomplished amazing things. How did we choose just these eighteen? We sought those who were visionary and who made choices that were not typical of their peers. Although there are many women who fit this profile, these eighteen represent different time periods, different ethnic backgrounds, and different professions. Their dedication and persistence make them role models for children today and their message is clear. Work hard. Stay the course.

Florence Elizabeth Riefle Bahr, 1909-1998

Artist and Activist

Florence Riefle Bahr

Florence Riefle Bahr loved art and she loved to paint. She carried sketchbooks with her at all times and in them she drew anything that caught her interest—be it a face of a fellow bus rider, a Baltimore row house, or a flower. As a young girl she delighted in creating cards and special mementoes for friends and family members. She also cared deeply for people and wanted to right the world's wrongs. Her family accepted that but they could not understand her participation in the Civil Rights marches and the Anti-Vietnam War demonstrations that took place in the United States in the 1960s and 1970s. At that time few Baltimore women joined such public displays and certainly not one who had been raised in a proper, upper-class Jewish family. Florence's notebooks were her diaries and in many of them she sketched scenes that documented the political upheaval of those two decades. Florence Bahr was a woman with an abundance of energy and a wide range of interests. She had compassion for her fellow man and she had the courage to act upon her beliefs.

Florence grew up in the Park Heights section of Baltimore City. Her grandfather, Henry F. Riefle, was a butcher and sold meat in Lexington Market, a downtown market where Baltimoreans could buy fresh fruit, vegetables, and meat cut to their specifications. When Florence was a teenager, her father, James Henry, or "Harry," as he was called, left his father's business and began to sell real estate. He did well buying and selling property and eventually he and his wife, Florence Shafer, moved their six children into one of the first houses in Homeland, another area of the city.

Florence's family followed the traditions of their native German heritage. The Riefles expected their children to adhere to standards that were typical of a family of their social class. There were two full time employees, a cook and gardener. Florence was aware of how socially conscious her parents were but she accepted it as a normal way of life. All the Riefles were accomplished musicians and frequently attended the symphony. Florence did play the piano, but she preferred to paint. This set her apart from the rest of the family and she was determined to excel as a visual artist.

After graduating from Forest Park High School in 1927, Florence went to Dickinson College in Carlisle, Pennsylvania. The academic side of college life did not interest her. She devoted much of her time to art classes and helped design the yearbook. Two years later she returned to Baltimore and entered the Maryland Institute of Mechanical Arts, now the Maryland Institute College of Art. She attended both day and night classes and received her diploma in Costume Design in 1930. In 1931 Florence received another diploma in Fine Arts and won the James Young Memorial Prize. The following year she received a diploma for Fine Arts in postgraduate studies.

While she mastered watercolor techniques at the Institute, she often looked out the window and watched a group of African American children playing in the nearby schoolyard. One day the children, including a little girl in her mother's polka dot dress, appeared in their parents' clothes. Florence became so enchanted with their game of make believe and the swirling polka dots that she sketched them. Inspired, she wrote a story and included it and the drawings in her first book, *The Polka-Dot Petticoat*. She wrote and illustrated more stories but never published them.

Florence met Leonard Bahr at the Institute. He was an older student who also taught a portraiture class. She caught his attention when she modeled for his class and their romance began. Florence's parents expressed reservations about their daughter's choice for a husband because Leonard did not have the same background or social standing that the Riefles did. The couple dated for four years before they married in 1934.

By the mid 1930s both Florence and Leonard began to receive recognition for their art. In 1935 the Baltimore Museum of Art invited Florence to exhibit her works and the following year the Maryland Institute sponsored a show highlighting paintings by both artists. Florence's entire family attended the exhibit and so did other art patrons. The guest book was full of many signatures.

The Baltimore Public Works Administration hired the couple to create murals for several public buildings and Florence designed one for the Harriet Lane Home for Invalid Children, part of the Johns Hopkins Hospital. In 1936 the National Association of Women Painters and Sculptors honored Florence by inviting her to join the organization. She had just begun to paint with oil, so she was delighted when the Association asked to exhibit *Lillie*, an oil portrait of the Riefle's family's cook, at its annual meeting in New York.

During World War II the couple lived in Florida while Leonard fulfilled his duty as a naval officer. When the Bahrs returned to Baltimore in 1946 they were a family of four. Leonard resumed his teaching post at the Maryland Institute and Florence focused on raising the children, Beth, Leonard, and a new daughter, Mary. They moved into Edgewood Cottage, an historic home on Old Lawyers' Hill Road in Elkridge, Maryland.

Their son, Len, wrote, "Lawyers' Hill was a lovely place to grow up, with heavily treed huge lots, old mansions, and little traffic. It was cooler than the city yet only about ten miles from downtown. Our old house had been built a century before, originally as a camp for 'escapees' from Baltimore summers."[1] He remembered that his father had reservations about the house because it needed many repairs. But it had a charm that appealed to his mother and she had the final word.

Years later, the Bahrs built a larger house on the property, which connected to a studio that had been built for Leonard earlier. In order for each of them to have a place to work, Florence claimed a sunny room near the kitchen for her studio. Mary remembered that before they left the old house, she and Len drew pictures on their bedroom walls and that he covered his ceiling with yellow, black, and orange horses. The Bahrs provided many activities that enriched their children's lives and Len said, "Life on Lawyers' Hill in the 1950s was never dull."[2] Their friends seemed to enjoy the offbeat atmosphere and lively conversations at the Bahr household.

While the children were growing up, Florence continued to explore different art mediums such as pencil, watercolor, charcoal, oil, ink, and lithography. Both Mary and

Len remembered going on outings with their mother as she searched for interesting objects to draw or use in her art. Mary said her mother liked to sketch old doors and that she often went with Florence and scouted Baltimore's alleys in search of unusual ones. Len recalled her love of nature and wrote, "Any unusual leaf or insect never escaped her interest and eventually became immortalized in a sketchbook."[3] She also created collages. One, called *Totem*, was an abstract composition of bird feathers, pieces of wood, pebbles, glass, and butterflies. She created another collage, *Homage to Rachel Carson*, in honor of the environmentalist.

Leonard and Florence enjoyed canoeing on the Magothy River. Florence rarely returned from these outings empty handed. Once she brought home a fish skeleton and despite its odor, she created a woodcut. She even saw beauty in cicadas, which appear in Maryland every seventeen years. Using only a part of this insect, she created a sculpture called, *Fragment*, which was exhibited in an art show. Another time she found a dead bird that she wanted to paint, but because she did not have time to do so at the moment, she put it in the freezer. This was a fairly common occurrence and did not surprise the family.

Although the children occupied much of her time, Florence continued to explore her artistic interests. She was a skilled seamstress and often made matching outfits for her children. Her reputation as a portrait painter grew and her favorite subjects were her own children. In 1948 the children's magazine, *Jack and Jill,* hired her to illustrate some of their stories. The Baltimore Health Department, local churches, and missionary groups commissioned her to design posters and other promotional materials. Many people asked her to create personalized greeting cards, invitations, and bookplates. She taught art classes to groups as well as individuals, always providing words of encouragement.

In 1964 Florence wanted to further her education. Not bothered about being older than the other students, she enrolled in Catonsville Community College. She took science courses and found that she was amazed by the colors and minute details she saw through a microscope. With her artistic eye, she found it exciting to discover something new each day and draw it. She returned to the Maryland Institute and received a master's degree in printmaking in 1967. She never lost her ambition to learn and to be the best at what she did.

Florence had great compassion for the less fortunate. She had always helped people but in conventional ways, through committees and organizations. But the turmoil of the 1960s and 1970s forced her to change. These were decades characterized by assassinations, riots, and demonstrations. President John F. Kennedy was killed in Dallas, Texas, in 1963 and Martin Luther King was assassinated in Memphis, Tennessee, in April 1968, and two months later, Robert Kennedy, John's younger brother, was killed in California after winning a Democratic primary. The Vietnam War and Civil Rights were the topics in newspapers all over the country. No longer satisfied at being a quiet supporter, Florence became an activist. She was the local representative for the Southern Christian Leadership Association, whose purpose was to organize protests in various cities. Wearing armbands and T-shirts, Florence joined protestors in the fight for desegregation. Both Mary and Len remembered accompanying her when she joined picket lines at Gwynn Oak Park.

When Martin Luther King, Jr. was assassinated, Florence became so grief stricken that she went to her studio and painted his image over and over. She filled sketchbooks with drawings of the slain leader along with words from his, "I Have a Dream" speech. On one page, she sketched his face imposed on the American Flag. She saved church programs from religious services for the Civil Rights leader along with relevant quotes from ministers. Clearly these events affected her deeply. She painted a large work titled, *An Homage to Martin Luther King, Jr.* Later she gave it to the headquarters for the National Association for the Advancement of Colored People in Baltimore.

Martin Luther King, by Florence Riefle Bahr

Other issues became prominent as a result of the openness of the Civil Rights movement. Native Americans and Hispanic farm workers felt that they had rights that should be acknowledged. Native Americans wanted to reclaim land the government had made them leave and migrant Mexican laborers wanted fair wages for seasonal grape picking in California. These causes did not escape Florence's attention. She went to rallies in Washington, DC, to support the Native Americans and in 1965 she gave money to Cesar Chavez, founder of the United Farm Workers Union. She created banners and posters for these causes as well.

Florence agreed with many other Americans that the United States did not belong in the Vietnam War and she participated in antiwar demonstrations. Once, a nephew who lived out of town went to Washington, DC, to protest the war and recognized his aunt among the crowd. Knowing that his parents were concerned about him, he called them after the rally to say that he was all right. When his parents told him to call his Auntie Flo if he needed help, he replied that she would not be much help because she was among the demonstrators. At another protest she documented the poor arrangements, the lack of direction, and how upset she was by the experience. Her frustration could be seen in the facial expressions she sketched of the demonstrators. But this did not stop her from joining future protests. In 1970 the Women's League for Peace and Freedom presented Florence with an award for her stand against the war and for the way she used art to support peace.

Children's welfare was also important to Florence. She served breakfasts to inner city youth for a program sponsored by another Civil Rights group active in the 1970s, the Black Panthers. Feeling that it was important that these young people know more than asphalt and concrete, she invited a young African American boy to spend time with her family at Lawyers' Hill, where he could share the same experiences her children had. However, they could not escape the prejudice against African Americans that people had. One Sunday, Florence took him to church. Despite the fact that Florence attended that church frequently, no one spoke to them. "…Florence never returned to worship at that particular church," [4] said her daughter, Mary.

Florence did not keep her opinions to herself. A firm believer in democracy, she wrote weekly letters to government officials, including the President of the United States, expressing ways to improve women's rights, provide better education for children, and better living conditions for prisoners. She became involved with the American Friends Service Committee, a Quaker group whose members supported peace. She encouraged others to get involved because she believed that many voices would increase the likelihood for change.

Florence served as a courtroom artist for the corruption trial of Maryland Governor Marvin Mandel in 1977. Her talent and good memory allowed her to capture the emotion and tension of the scene. She sympathized with Daniel and Phillip Berrigan and documented the Catonsville Nine trial, when nine Jesuit priests, including the Berrigan brothers, were accused of burning draft records to protest the Vietnam War. She sketched the backs of people's heads in the courtroom as well as jurors whose faces showed intense concentration. The drawings included the jurors' names and Florence's reactions to the questions lawyers asked.

In the 1980s Florence opened the Humpty Dumpty Museum in Ellicott City, a small town near her home. This would be a showcase for her doll collection. When she was a young girl, her parents and relatives gave her dolls from Germany, several made in the 1800s. Over time she added to the collection. The museum's name reflected a promise that she made to herself that if she ever owned a store, she would name it after the Humpty Dumpty doll she purchased years earlier at a Goodwill Store. Although she sold antiques and dolls, her greatest joy was giving tours of her private collection, which often lasted up to two hours. Mary remembered that her mother felt that dolls were one way to interpret social history and that she emphasized this as she described each doll's origin. If she was not giving tours, she painted watercolors of the dolls. She planned to make a book of these illustrations but never did.

In 1996 The Peabody Galleria Piccola exhibited much of Florence's art. On display were her early paintings of Baltimore row houses, portraits, lithographs, collages, and sculptures. Art admirers, former students, and many others crowded the exhibit. What had been planned as a single day event, continued for two days. People wanted to buy her art and they wanted to see her notebooks. Florence was reluctant to put prices on items and those that she did were ridiculously low. That prompted a protest from the curator who told Florence that she should put a higher price on her works. Florence was hesitant, and as a result the curator priced the items as best she could, but certainly at a higher price than Florence would have.

Florence remained in the house on Lawyers' Hill after Leonard died. Her children were concerned about her living alone, but Florence refused to move. She was an avid reader and over the years she had accumulated thousands of books. She had created numerous files that contained articles and information that she thought might be useful in the future. There was little time for Florence to produce more work. She died from smoke inhalation when her house caught fire in 1998. Her son Len wrote, "She would not have agreed to live anywhere else but surrounded by her treasures, lovingly collected over a lifetime."[5]

People remembered Florence Bahr as a talented artist. The Maryland Archives have acquired some of her sketchbooks and museums and private collectors have obtained some of her art. People also remembered her as one who did her best to make things better for mankind. She was a spiritual person who worked toward peace and she abhorred the cruelty and the lack of concern and compassion that she saw in the world. Her sketchbooks from the 1960s and 1970s left a visual record of a place in time in the history of the United States as seen through Florence Bahr's eyes. Art provided her a way to express her feelings and she used her talent to share what she saw. Her drawings, as well as the inserted newspaper clippings, invitations, and announcements in her sketchbooks reflected her varied interests.

Posthumously, in 1999, she was the first artist inducted into the Maryland Women's Hall of Fame.

Helen Delich Bentley, 1923-
Reporter and US Congresswoman

Helen Delich Bentley

What were the odds that a baby girl born in the mining town of Ruth, Nevada, in 1923 would serve Maryland's Second Congressional District in the US House of Representatives for five terms? Or that she would be one of the first women to travel overnight on a Navy warship and would have the entire port of Baltimore, Maryland, named in her honor? The story of Helen Delich Bentley had more to do with hard work and determination than with Lady Luck, but Mrs. Bentley said she lived in a gambling atmosphere all her life.

The story began when Mary Bjelich came from Yugoslavia to join her husband in the United States in 1906. Her journey on the ship took more than a month, and she spent most of her time below deck. It was cramped and uncomfortable. It was a relief when the ship finally docked in Baltimore. Mary and her husband traveled north at once to Harrisburg, Pennsylvania, where he got a job working in a coal mine. Unfortunately, the job was difficult and dangerous, and young Sam Bjelich, like many other miners in those days, died there in a mining accident. Mary was alone.

She had no money and she had little understanding of English. There was no reason she could see to stay in Harrisburg. She was ready to give up and return to Yugoslavia when another miner, Mane Ivanesevich, convinced her not to leave. He and Mary married and he chose Delich as his American name. At about that time the Pennsylvania mine where he worked was closing and miners were looking for work in other states. The young couple were in Arizona in 1909, when their first daughter was born, and work had them shuttling between copper mines in Arizona and Nevada for several years.

By 1917 the family settled down in the small town of Ruth, Nevada. This was the home of the Nevada Consolidated Copper Company. Helen, born in 1923, was the youngest of their seven children. Two of her brothers died in childhood, one in infancy and another brother, who was very close to her, died of infected tonsils at age twelve. At that time there were no drugs available to help him.

The town of Ruth, named for the copper mine owner's daughter, was first settled in 1903. It was a company town, where the company ran the town administration and also owned the houses, which it rented to the miners. However, Helen and her family were considered "foreigners" and were not allowed to rent a company house. They lived apart from the other miners and their houses were cramped and poor. They had no running water and women had to carry water from the street into their houses each day.

After some time, another section of Ruth became available to the "foreigners" and the Delichs moved. Most of the families were of Mediterranean descent, with many Greeks, Italians, and Slavs. The Novack family and the Popoviches were their neighbors. The children played together in the Tonopah Canyon and Helen recalled that Adam Popovich and his brothers, talented singers, became successful musicians in Chicago when they were older.

Ruth and Kimberly were small towns in eastern Nevada. The county seat, Ely, was a bit larger. Each town had a small Catholic church and there were Mormon and Orthodox churches nearby. Stores in each town sold necessities and many of them offered gambling and games of chance as well.

Helen's family built a house in Ruth. To help pay their expenses her mother took in boarders, with the men "hot-bunking." While one man slept, a second man worked a shift at the mine, and at the end of the shift the men switched places. Bed sheets for the boarders and for the family were made from empty Portland Cement bags, and changing those sheets was one of Helen's jobs.

In 1932 Helen's father was stricken with miner's consumption, a lung disease. He was sick for months, and there was no medical help for him. She was eight years old when he died. The income from the boarders helped them survive financially after her father's death. Many of the boarders were from Yugoslavia, and they enriched Helen's life as well, sharing their country's stories and legends with her.

The Great Depression made times worse. Even families who had men with steady jobs in the mine struggled to make ends meet. Trains carried copper from underground to the smelter in McGill, Nevada, and people heated their houses with bits of coal the children picked up from the train track beds. Families struggled to provide the most basic food, clothing, and shelter.

Helen's mother had gone only through the fifth grade in school in Yugoslavia, and she had had to teach herself English when she came to the United States. She now read widely and she expected her children to do so, too. The company maintained a small library called "The Clubhouse," and the family made good use of it. Mary was very emphatic; her children would take advantage of education. "I wanted to learn," remembered Helen, "and Mom always encouraged me."[1] She went to grammar school in Ruth, where her teachers were conscientious and capable. Elementary teacher Maria Buckmaster was "an exact person" who emphasized proper English and penmanship. Helen also credited her high school teachers in Ely with developing her ability with language.

Helen Delich flourished in high school. She took part in oratorical contests and debates, wrote with increasing skill, and "read everything I could get my hands on."[2] In 1941 she won the Elks National Scholarship for Girls, an award of $500. She flew to Philadelphia to attend the awards ceremony. The flight was not direct and she had to make several changes along the way. She was also awarded a grant from the Serbian National Federation. She would have liked to study law, but she knew she could not afford the years of study that a law degree would require. Helen attended the University of Nevada for one year and worked in the Extension Service Office.

Next she enrolled in The University of Missouri to study journalism. Her love of words, reading, speaking, and writing made this a good choice. To help pay her way she worked at King's Drugstore, earning ten cents an hour. Later she worked in the University dining center, where she earned thirty cents an hour and had three free meals. The journalism courses, she felt, were useful. They led to an offer to go to Washington, DC, to work in Senator Jim Scrugham's office while she studied at George Washington University. This lasted only one semester. "I hated politics!" she exclaimed, "and wanted nothing to do with it!"[3]

Helen returned to Missouri, where she worked as a stringer for United Press. A stringer is a freelance journalist paid for each piece of writing rather than being on the pay roll. She continued her studies and finished her degree in September 1944. Mary could not attend the graduation ceremony because, on the same day, she had a ceremony of her own to attend. On the day Helen Delich received her Bachelors degree, her mother, Mary, became a citizen of the United States.

Helen was offered a journalism job in Indianapolis, IN, and she set a fast pace. After three weeks she was asked to go to Fort Wayne to run the office there. Writing for their weekly newsletter, *The Red Letter,* which contained many filler-type stories that could be published at any time, Helen produced more than anyone else. Her skills and her reputation as a good reporter were growing, and soon other newspapers wanted to hire her. Helen next set her sights on the East Coast. She wrote all the larger eastern papers she knew of and asked for a job as a reporter on any beat other than the women's or society pages. The *Louisville Courier* offered her a job on its copy desk, and she was almost ready to accept when another offer came in. *The Baltimore Sun* wanted to hire her as a reporter. They offered her $5 more than *The Courier* and would also pay her transportation to Baltimore. Helen was on her way to Maryland.

She arrived in Baltimore in June 1945, at about the time when the Second World War was coming to an end. Labor unions were active and Helen, working alongside the *Sun's* chief labor writer, Herbert Bradley, learned about labor issues. When Mr. Bradley moved on the following year she took over his responsibilities. Being a woman in that job was difficult, but once people understood she was a no-nonsense person, she said, she earned the respect of her colleagues. When the war ended and men returned from the armed forces to their former jobs, only three women reporters remained at *The Baltimore Sun*. Helen was one. In 1948 she was assigned to cover news on the waterfront of Baltimore's port, and she was named Maritime Editor of *The Sun* in 1953. She was the only woman to hold that post at a major US newspaper. She was a long way from the women's section.

She went at her assignment with typical drive and determination and taught herself what she needed to know about shipping and transportation. As she learned about the activities in the port, she began to understand what was needed to help the Port of Baltimore grow and thrive in a competitive industry. Early in her assignment, in October of 1945, to help publicize Navy Week, she persuaded the Navy to let her sail overnight from Norfolk to Baltimore on the USS Randolph. The idea of having a woman aboard a Navy warship for such a trip was shocking to many people, including the ship's crew. Brought aboard in a boatswain's chair, she enjoyed the trip, but the Navy, uneasy over the public's reaction to a woman spending the night on a Navy ship, refused to acknowledge the story for several years.

Her column, "Around the Waterfront," ran three times a week in *The Baltimore Sun* and was nationally syndicated. Helen continued to pursue stories about the port and its city and paid special attention to its many unique residents. She wrote of Bob McCurdy, superintendent of the Hercules Company, which cleaned ships' holds, tanks, and hulls. She described his responsibilities for checking jobs in progress and bidding on new business. She profiled Nicholas Mitrov, who sold ship supplies around the port and spoke nine different languages. She wrote of the Meisel family, who sold supplies to the sailors, and she wrote about Bettye Mills, owner of the city's Stork Club. She wrote about Rex Wheeler, the youngest steamship manager in the port, and spoke of his concern that the Baltimore business community did not do enough to actively promote the port.

As time went on, promoting the port and its potential became her personal mission. In 1951 she began a job that would raise the profile of the port, creating, producing, and hosting the weekly television series, *The Port That Built A City And A State.* That program ran for fifteen years and covered more than 200 port-oriented subjects. Its purpose was to help people see the importance of shipping and international trade, and to highlight the many facets of the port itself. An estimate showed approximately 10,000 people were in jobs associated with the waterfront. Some of the television programs focused on those people, such as tugboat captains, longshoremen, and divers. Other programs concentrated on the ships themselves, how they were built, how repairs were made, and how cargo was stowed efficiently. Training and skills necessary to operate ships were covered as well, including details on becoming a merchant seaman, how to tie proper knots, and how to board a ship. Still other programs showed the amazing variety of cargo that passed through the harbor. Just a few examples of that variety were sugar and coffee, tea, cars, trucks, coal, umbrellas, wallboard, paint, broom handles, and steel. More than 100 companies were involved in importing and exporting through the Port of Baltimore. The unique program was widely celebrated and Helen Delich earned praise for her knowledge and vision.

Using both the television series and her *Sun* columns, Helen gradually pushed for the creation of the Maryland Port Authority, which would give Maryland the chance to compete vigorously for jobs and cargo. She continued to learn more about the business of the port, kept detailed lists of ways to emphasize and publicize its value, and gained respect for her knowledge. Her influence was growing.

Helen held her own anywhere in the port, and her use of direct language was a surprise to those meeting her for the first time. But she did not neglect what would now, be called her "feminine side." She was well known for her attention to her appearance, and stories say that when she walked into the newsroom other reporters stopped typing and looked up to see what she was wearing. She was stylish and led an active social life. She believed in the value of good-quality textiles, and in the careful design and construction of clothing. During the late winter of 1959, Helen called a friend saying she needed an escort for a party that night. The friend introduced Helen to her brother, Bill Bentley, a Baltimore teacher. Helen Delich and Bill Bentley were married the following June.

Helen Delich Bentley's knowledge and her ability to get things done kept growing. She was mentioned as a possible nominee for a number of federal appointments but was rejected, quite possibly because she was a woman. Therefore, when she was finally offered a seat on the Federal Maritime Commission, she insisted that she would accept the offer only if she was named chairman. President Richard Nixon appointed her to that post in 1969.

The Maritime Commission's responsibilities included regulating ocean freight rates, licenses, and commercial shipping agreements. Helen went to work to make people aware of the importance of the Commission. From her days at *The Baltimore*

Sun and her efforts on behalf of Baltimore's port, she had many contacts within the industry. Moreover, she had a solid understanding of labor issues. She understood and appreciated maritime trade issues and was able to speak directly and to the point on these subjects. Described as unconventional and as one who disliked wasting time, she addressed problems head-on and could work swiftly and behind the scenes to resolve disputes. Her sometimes informal approach made some people nervous, but her voice was clear and unequivocal as she spoke for the transportation industry in Washington and at international forums. She was instrumental in dealing with the Soviet Union on Atlantic trade rates. She was alert to the emerging development of containership commerce and understood that its impact would be enormous. She brought common sense to her decisions as well. For instance, at her insistence, the Military Sea Transportation Service, which was on the verge of being given to the Army, was kept under Navy jurisdiction. The work was intense and her determination to do a good job was important to the commission's work but tiring to Helen. She resigned in 1975 and began work as an international consultant on maritime commerce and trade issues.

Her commitment to the Port of Baltimore led her back into government. By 1982 it was clear that the future of shipping for the Port of Baltimore depended on its ability to handle container ships. Those ships required deep water. A bill that would provide for the dredging of a 50-foot-deep channel in the port had been held up in Congress for more than ten years. Helen ran for Congress first in 1982, when she lost the race, and again in 1984, when she won. A tireless and decisive advocate for the port, she campaigned for the passage of a bill to dredge the needed channels. The bill passed, the port was dredged, and Helen Bentley continued to serve in the House of Representatives for five terms from 1985 to 1995. During her time in Congress, she focused on constituent services, industrial and manufacturing matters, and maritime issues. She served on the Appropriations Committee as well as the Budget, Public Works and Transportation, and Merchant Marine and Fisheries Committees as well.

By 2007 the Port of Baltimore was visited by approximately 2,300 large, deep-sea vessels and was ranked first in the country in handling Roll On /Roll Off cargo. It covered 45 miles of waterfront and was one of the most successful ports in the country. Mrs. Bentley remained its ardent advocate and supporter and, always looking ahead, said it needs land, storage, and a new 50-foot berth to handle larger container ships.

When Governor Robert Ehrlich announced in 2006 that the Port would be named in her honor, Mrs. Bentley said she was speechless—a rare state for an eloquent and determined woman whose dedication helped build the Helen Delich Bentley Port of Baltimore.

Margaret Brent, 1602-1671

Landowner

Margaret Brent was born into an upper-middle class family in Gloucestershire, England, in 1601. A daughter born into a family like hers was usually expected to live at home with her parents until she married, keeping herself busy with needlework and other gentle pursuits. Margaret did not follow that path. She would sail across the Atlantic Ocean to the new colony, Maryland, establish herself in Saint Mary's City society, and make her own living trading land, tobacco, and indentured servants. She ably represented herself in courts of law and caught the attention of Governor Leonard Calvert, who would choose her to be the executor of his estate. She worked with exceptional skill to fulfill her responsibilities, and her management of his estate helped save a colony that was close to failure.

At the time of Margaret's birth, Queen Elizabeth I was in the final years of her reign as Queen of England. Elizabeth appreciated the arts, and they flourished when she was on the throne. In the relative peace of late Elizabethan England, the decorative arts prospered. Paintings, especially miniature portraits, were prized. Textiles were produced by hand and were often luxurious. But from the beginning of Elizabeth's reign the well being of Roman Catholics in England was uncertain. Elizabeth herself was not a Catholic, and the Puritans were growing in numbers and in strength. They were not supporters of the Catholics.

James I followed Elizabeth on the throne. During his reign, Shakespeare published his First Folio and the Globe Theatre burned to the ground during a performance of *Henry VIII* when its thatched roof was ignited by a cannon ball. The Anglican Church's *King James Bible* was published in 1611, and in 1620 the Mayflower sailed from Plymouth, carrying a small and determined band of Puritans who would form a new settlement in America. It was an interesting and exciting time.

Not everyone in England thrived during this time. Richard and Elizabeth Brent were members of the upper-middle class and were distant cousins of the prominent Calvert family. They were also Roman Catholics, who were not in favor during the reigns of Elizabeth, James, or, later, that of Charles I. The Brent family did not have an easy time raising their thirteen children.

Cecil Calvert, the second Lord Baltimore, wanted to establish a place in the New World where Catholics would be welcomed, but he did not want to limit the new colony to those who shared his faith. To encourage non-Catholics to settle in his colony, he promised religious tolerance for all Christian faiths. He appointed his brother, Leonard, as governor. It was to this new colony, Maryland, that Margaret Brent, her sister Mary, and their brothers, Giles and Fulke, decided to emigrate.

The four Brents arrived in Maryland in 1638. Margaret and her sister Mary brought a letter from Lord Baltimore asking the governor that they be granted land on favorable terms. They brought a number of servants and enough money to begin acquiring property. With the help of Lord Baltimore's letter they were able to set up their own household on 70 acres in Saint Mary's City, the colony's capital. They named their new home *Sisters Freehold*.

The majority of the settlers in Maryland were men; there were very few women. Margaret was in an unusual and favorable position. As an unmarried woman she was allowed to own and to manage property; however, if she married, her property would be given to her husband and she would lose the right to control it. As long as she stayed single, she remained in charge of her assets.

Margaret went to work. She bought and sold indentured servants, lent money to new arrivals in the colony, and went to court to collect the debts owed to her. With experience she became an able businesswoman, and others came to admire and respect her talents. She planned for the future, as well as thinking of the present, and she bought a 1,000-acre parcel of land on Kent Island in addition to her land in St. Mary's City.

Even as Maryland and Margaret Brent flourished, events in England were spilling over that would cause a crisis in the colony. Charles I, who became King in 1625, was known as a strong and determined leader. Disputes within his government led to a Civil War in England in 1642, and the effects of that war spread to Maryland. In 1645 a revolt by Protestant settlers forced Governor Leonard Calvert, a Catholic, to flee to Virginia and many colonists fled with him. The population of Maryland dropped dramatically. The rebels invaded Saint Mary's City, destroyed property that belonged to Catholics, and captured two Jesuit priests and Margaret's brother Giles. They put the men in chains and sent them to England on a ship. Few people remained in Maryland, and the colony was on the edge of collapse.

After approximately one year, Leonard Calvert returned from Virginia with a small army of hired soldiers and was able to take back control of the colony. By that time few rebels remained to fight against his forces, and Calvert won those people over by promising to pardon everyone who would swear allegiance to Lord Baltimore. The future seemed brighter until six months later when Leonard Calvert suddenly became ill and died. This was another blow to the Brents because their prosperity depended in part on their relationship to the Calvert family. On his deathbed Calvert named Thomas Green as governor of Maryland and chose Margaret Brent as his sole executor. He did not explain his choice. He had observed her for several years as she handled her own business affairs and had confidence in her abilities. The fact that she was his cousin, even though a distant one, may have influenced him. It would be her job to settle all of Calvert's debts, and his debts were substantial.

She would have a great deal of trouble paying those people he owed. When he engaged the army to help him retake the colony of Maryland, rather than arranging to have the government pay them, Leonard Calvert had pledged to pay the men himself. At the end of the rebellion, the colony was in serious disorder. More than half the settlers had abandoned their homes and fled to nearby Virginia, where life was peaceful. Food was in short supply, and the soldiers hired by Leonard Calvert were hungry, angry, and impatient. They went to Margaret Brent, as Calvert's representative, and demanded their pay. Historians estimated that each man was owed 1,500 pounds of tobacco and three barrels of corn. Officers would be paid more. Under English law, which governed the colony, Margaret could not sell Calvert's land or buildings to satisfy his debts. She did use all his other assets to help pay his soldiers, but there was not enough money to settle all the claims.

She knew the Maryland Assembly would not agree to pay the soldiers that Governor Calvert had said he himself would pay. The men who were still waiting for their earnings were furious and close to revolt, and the colony's survival depended on her skill in dealing with them. She did her best to calm the soldiers and negotiate. In early January 1648, the Provincial Court finally appointed her as Lord Baltimore's legal representative. She pressed the Court further when on January 21, 1648, she demanded she be allowed not just one, but two votes in the Assembly. Her argument was that she should have one vote as a landowner and a second vote as Lord Baltimore's representative. When the Court refused her request she protested the decision, and then she went right to work selling Lord Baltimore's cattle to satisfy the soldiers' claims against his brother's estate. If she was to bring the issue of the soldiers' pay to a calm resolution, she had no choice but to sell his cattle. With peace restored, and the demand for tobacco increasing, the Maryland colony began to grow rapidly.

However, the sale of his cattle angered Lord Baltimore, who may have misunderstood or mistrusted Margaret's motives. Members of the Assembly wrote him supporting and praising her actions. They pointed out her courage in making difficult choices, and her tact and grace in dealing with the angry soldiers. They felt that she, more than any other person, was responsible for the safety and well-being of the colony. Her gentle, feminine instincts and her skill in negotiating were key factors in the preservation of the colony of Maryland. They pointed out that most of his cattle had been seized by the rebels early in the uprising and only about a dozen were left for Margaret to sell to pay the soldiers. Lord Baltimore remained unmoved. The loss of his confidence was difficult for her because the close alliance with the Calvert family had been important to Margaret and the rest of the Brent family.

Added to this, the appointment of a new Protestant governor made the prospect of continuing to live in Maryland uncomfortable. So Margaret Brent, whose skill and determination helped save a colony, moved to the Northern Neck of Virginia to a plantation she named "Peace." She died there in 1671, and left most of her property in Maryland and Virginia to her brother Giles and his children. Her legacy was one of courage; she had the wisdom to see what needed to be done and the willingness to persist. Her actions helped ensure that the colony of Maryland would survive and flourish.

Anna Ella Carroll, 1815-1894
Political Activist

Anna Ella Carroll was born into one of Maryland's leading families on August 29, 1815. A daughter of such a family at that time was expected to master the feminine arts of needlework, art, and music; to marry well; and then run her own household gracefully and with little obvious effort. Anna Ella Carroll did not follow this script. As an adult she claimed she knew how to sew, although a younger sister declared Anna never so much as held a needle in her hand. She never married, and she would later insist she was the author of a major military campaign in the Civil War, and that she was an unrecognized member of Abraham Lincoln's Cabinet.

Her father, Thomas King Carroll, was a cousin of Charles Carroll, a signer of the Declaration of Independence. He inherited his Somerset County plantation, Kingston Hall, in1814, about the time he married the beautiful Julianna Stevenson of Baltimore. The house to which he brought his bride was a typical Maryland plantation home, with a central section flanked by two wings. It was generous in size, with more than 20 rooms and 40 windows. Looking out those windows Julianna could see the large and handsome lawns and gardens that ran down to the Annemessex River. The furnishings were rich, the doorknobs were brass, and the rugs were from the Orient. The main crop was tobacco, and more than one hundred enslaved men and women did the work on the plantation. Like neighboring families, the young Carrolls looked forward to a life that they expected would have an easy rhythm and would be comfortably free from care.

Anna Ella, their first child, had five sisters and two brothers, but "Miss Anne" would be her father's favorite child. He educated her as he would a son. Under his direction, she studied literature, philosophy, and law by reading Coke and Blackburn, Kant, and Shakespeare. She treasured the time she spent with her father discussing these works. She practiced the domestic arts but she was much more interested in books. The household had frequent visitors. Ladies and their children paid calls on the women of the Carroll family, and from these occasions, Anna learned the fine points of friendly conversation and she absorbed many social graces that would be very helpful to her years later. Men came to call on her father to discuss issues of politics and government, economics, slavery, and states' rights. Anna was fascinated by their earnest talk.

Thomas Carroll did not like the institution of slavery, but when he inherited Kingston Hall it had a substantial number of slaves. He did not feel freed slaves had a proper place in a slave-owning society, so he could not bring himself to free them. Neither would he consider selling them, for it was likely they would be sold into much less favorable conditions than he could offer them. He felt his best path was to work to make Kingston Hall a thriving plantation so that both his own family and his slaves would have a good life. He would struggle with this concern for years.

He had an interest in government, served in the state House of Delegates in 1816 and 1817, and was elected Governor in 1829. During the first winter, he went to Annapolis by himself, leaving Julianna and the children at home in the country. Anna found this dull. She missed him and wrote him many flowery letters. The next year, according to one source, the family went to Annapolis together, traveling nearly 70 miles in carriages from home to the ferry dock. Anna and her parents were in the lead carriage, and accepted occasional bouquets of flowers from villagers as they passed through town. Young Anna was reported to enjoy the trip. Her family enrolled her at a boarding school run by Ms. Margaret Mercer in West River, Maryland. Ms. Mercer, like Anne, was the daughter of a Maryland governor and had also been taught by her father. Her school understood the necessity of a young woman learning to be a lady and did teach the womanly arts, but it also instructed Anna in science, philosophy, ethics, and religion. This was more to Anna's liking.

At the end of his term as governor, Thomas Carroll returned home hoping to make his plantation more successful. It was a struggle. A recession from 1819 to 1822 had weakened the family finances, taxes had increased, transportation was a problem, and the soil was overworked and tired. Further, as more babies were born to the slave families at Kingston Hall, the cost of running the plantation rose higher and higher. But Anna was pleased to have her father back at home. While ladies continued to pay social calls upon her mother, once her father returned, many men came to visit him to discuss the latest news in politics and government. Anne acted as her father's ally and spy. She was sociable and pleasant to the women who came to exchange news with her mother and would listen carefully to them. Then she went to her father to pass on bits of information and to tell him what subjects the women had discussed. Thus Anne practiced her social skills at the same time she learned more about politics and government.

The battle to make Kingston Hall successful became more and more difficult. Farming was demanding and complex, and Anna's father was a poor manager of both farming and finances. Her father's "generosity" was the problem, she said. He was forced to sell off all but seven family slaves, and Anna went to New York City to ask for help from leading abolitionists and philanthropists. She raised $4,000 and arranged for the slaves to be freed. Then her father mortgaged all the household goods. Judgments and lawsuits were brought against him for debts he owed, and he was unable to pay them. In 1837, when a monetary panic swept the country, Thomas Carroll lost Kingston Hall. He tried other careers, including law and insurance, in an attempt to support his family, but he did not succeed at any of them.

His failure brought out a new side of his eldest daughter. Anna, now twenty-two, rented a house and started a school to help support her family. By 1840 it appeared to be prospering, with twenty students studying under Ms. Carroll's direction, but that good fortune would not last. In 1843 money problems forced her to close the school. She moved again, first to Dorchester County and then to Baltimore.

It was in Baltimore that she began to build on two of her greatest strengths: her understanding of the power of language and her ability to persuade people to accept her. She set to work as a writer, composing letters and short commentaries on political issues. Drawing on what she had learned from the discussions between her father and his friends, she wrote tirelessly, and local papers published her pieces and paid her for them. She did not hesitate to contact people she had met through her father and she began to travel frequently from Baltimore to the nation's capital, continuing to write and finding clients to pay her for her work. Because of her background she was quick to grasp many facets of the important issues, and her skill in social situations served her very well. She was welcomed into many circles and took full advantage of that welcome. At that time few women expressed their opinions about the subjects Anna tackled; they were not allowed to vote, and they were not expected to have any interest in "the affairs of men."

After her mother became ill and died in 1849, Anna invited her father to join her in Baltimore. At Anna's request he was given a job as a naval officer, and this success appeared to encourage her to take more advantage of her family's name, her background, and her perceived social status. She continued writing, but chose her subjects with care. She ignored typical women's issues, like women's rights, and focused clearly on the broad and politically important arguments. She began to ask her new acquaintances, and then to demand, that her friends be appointed to certain jobs within government, and when she asked she made sure to ask the most senior person she knew, not someone of lesser influence. Her phrases were often flowery, she was quick to use flattery and often signed letters, "Your best little friend," playing on her femininity. Frequently she was able to arrange an appointment for a friend or relative. If she was not successful the first time she simply tried again.

By 1855 the Whig party was in decline and the American Party, or Know-Nothings, controlled the Maryland Legislature. Anna thought they would become nationally popular. If she supported them now and their popularity increased, she believed she could make certain her father was financially secure. Then she came under the influence of Dr. Robert Breckinridge, the minister of the Second Presbyterian Church in Baltimore. He delivered angry speeches against foreigners and Roman Catholics, and his accusations were helpful to her. She wanted someone or something to blame for the difficulties in her life. The Catholic Church was a fine target. In 1856 Anna published *The Great American Battle*, in which she detailed the dangers she claimed were coming from the church and she had copies delivered to many newspapers. She suspected that the Postmaster General, who was a Catholic, had interfered with their delivery when some editors did not write letters of thanks to her. Her message appealed to the Know-Nothings.

In 1855 Anna spoke to Millard Fillmore, who was Zachary Taylor's Vice President, and became President in 1850 when Taylor died unexpectedly. She told Fillmore that he was being considered as a presidential candidate for the Know-Nothing Party, and she hinted that she could influence the Party's decision. By the time he was chosen to run, she appeared to believe that she was responsible for his nomination. Throughout the campaign she continued to write in support of him, and when the election was held and he won the state of Maryland, she was quick to take credit for that success. However, he came in third nationally. Anna's explanation was that not enough men listened to her. After the election she badgered Fillmore with letters complaining that he had not thanked her for her efforts during the campaign. When he wrote to apologize and to thank her, she reworded his letter and used it as a tribute to her, inviting others to attend a testimonial dinner given in her honor by the American Party. Subsequently Fillmore wrote to her asking her to return his letters. She said she was too busy, that she had only kept two or three of them, and she saw no reason for him to be angry since she had done much more for him than he had done for her.

When it was clear the Know-Nothings had lost power, Anna turned her attention to the Republicans. In the contest for president, she supported the candidacy of John Botts, a Virginian who was pro-Union. The North and South were on the verge of breaking completely apart. She understood the vital importance of this election, and she believed Botts could unite the country. He could also be her ticket back into a place of power and influence. But Botts would not agree to the Party platform against the extension of slavery. Anna was increasingly uneasy. Her candidate was not doing well, her family's money troubles continued, and she herself was beginning to go deaf. She proposed Judge John McLean, who was seventy-five, for President and Botts for his Vice President. Her strategy did not work. On May 18, 1860, the Republicans nominated Abraham Lincoln.

Anna did not know him. Her family continued to need her help and her friends were asking her to use her influence to find them jobs. Anna became ill in June and did not recover until September. By that time her sister Julianna had died, and so had a very close friend, John Causin, a former Maryland Legislature representative from St. Mary's County. His family wrote Anna and kindly offered to return letters she had written to him. She accepted their offer.

There was a very real possibility that Maryland would secede from the Union. Anna hoped desperately that would not happen. She understood that if Maryland seceded, Washington, DC, would be cut off from the northern states. Governor Thomas Hicks was a supporter of slavery and saw himself as a southerner, yet he was a friend of the Carroll family. He resisted when many citizens demanded a special legislative session, noting it would be costly and winter weather was a problem. He calmly asked Marylanders to wait for Lincoln's inauguration to see what other states and the Congress would do. Anna wrote frequently to newspapers praising his thoughtful, considered approach.

Then she turned her attention back to matters of patronage. Although she had not supported Lincoln in the election, now that he was in office she saw no problem in demanding favors and special consideration from the President and those in his administration, based on what she believed was her friendship with Lincoln. She pressed for two Cabinet appointments, neither of which came to be. She asked Thurlow Weed to contact Secretary of State Seward to appoint her father to the Naval Office in Baltimore. Apparently he did not do so. Then she complained to John Botts, who refused to interfere. In the midst of this, Governor Hicks called the Legislature into session to deal with the question of secession. The state of Maryland decided to stay with the Union.

With the Civil War underway, Anna wrote countless letters and pamphlets. She supported the Union but respectfully disagreed with Lincoln about forced emancipation, and she was clear and specific in her arguments. She urged him to consider colonization, moving freed slaves to another country, and she claimed she had a private meeting with him during which he asked her to point out a suitable spot on a map. She continued to write in support of the Union and in her "Reply to Breckenridge," she spoke out against Southeners who were anti-Lincoln. Senator Samuel Breckenridge was the leader of this group who supported a nation divided. Her letter was well received. She sent copies to the Secretary of the Interior, the Attorney General, and the President himself. She then printed 10,000 copies to distribute in Border States, where many people might be wavering. It was partly a generous thing for her to do, but also was meant to nudge the War Department to hire her to write for them. After meeting with an Assistant Secretary of War she came away happily convinced that as long as he approved her writing, his office would pay all costs. Later Breckenridge, a Senator from Kentucky and a former Vice President of the country, would openly join the Confederate sympathizers and would be expelled from the Senate.

And then came the Tennessee River Campaign. President Lincoln and many others believed the Union must get control of the Mississippi River. The war was not going well for the Union, and the country's leaders were anxious to have a major success. Members of the administration proposed a strategy they called the Anaconda plan. They would use gunboats to blockade the Mississippi so the South could not move goods along it. But it would be difficult to put the North's gunboats into place, and the Confederates had already fortified the river at many points. Anna said that when she was visiting in St. Louis, she happened to meet and talk with a riverboat pilot, Captain Charles Scott. He told her the Tennessee River, just a few miles east of the Mississippi, was deep enough for Union gunboats, was navigable all year, and was mostly unprotected by Confederate forts. Anna promptly wrote to Thomas Scott, the Assistant Secretary of War, and to President Lincoln proposing that rather than sailing up the fortified Mississippi, Union gunboats sail north on the Tennessee River. If a gunboat became disabled on that river, the current would take it back where it came from, and so it could avoid being captured. The plan was followed, and by February 1862, forts along the river had been captured and Nashville surrendered. This led to the Battle of Shiloh in early April, and the Confederacy was cut in two. When the Union was saved, Anna Ella Carroll felt it survived at least in part because of her plan. She continued to write letters to Lincoln, Scott, Secretary Stanton, and others, and her letters were often full of details and suggestions. Although she had no acknowledged place in the running of the country, she continued to offer her opinions to those who were in charge. In Francis Carpenter's famous painting of Lincoln's Cabinet, the artist included an empty chair. Anna claimed that chair was hers.

It seems unlikely that no one else had noticed the deep, easily navigable Tennessee River until Anna happened to visit St. Louis. In fact, Union forces had been at work on both it and the Cumberland River well before Anna met Captain Scott. That she recognized the importance of the river, and that she made sure the Union's leaders knew about it, were both to her credit. But her claim that the idea of using the Tennessee River was hers alone appeared more vain and foolish than factual. In spite of that, she spent years petitioning Congress for payment for the idea, and in her last years she continued to press for recognition and praise. In the end, Congress authorized payment of $2,000 for her writing during the war. It awarded her nothing for the Tennessee Campaign

Anna Ella Carroll lived with her sister Mary in Washington during the last years of her life. She was in poor health much of the time and died on February 19, 1894. Feminists have celebrated her story as the sad tale of a wronged woman. On the other side, anti-feminists might see her as an example of a woman gone wrong. Today she might well be both admired as a go-getter and looked down on as a selfish and self-serving person. Her truth would seem to lie somewhere in the middle. At the least, she was a woman brought up to lead a privileged life who suddenly lost all those privileges at age twenty-two. From that time on she lived by her wits, acted as her family's leader, and helped her friends whenever she could. From her father she learned the importance and excitement of politics and government. From her mother she learned the womanly arts. With those skills she fashioned a notable life's work of political activism at a time when women were not allowed to vote and few of them took an active interest in public affairs. She took charge and persevered, making a way for herself in the highest levels of government and society. She was indeed a remarkable woman.

Eugenie Clark, 1922-
Ichthyologist

Unraveling mysteries below the sea was an ongoing passion for Eugenie Clark. "I just love riddles, especially when they deal with fish,"[1] she said. Her curiosity was still as eager at age eighty-five as it was at five. A few days after her birthday in May 2007, Eugenie Clark flew to New Guinea to spend six months studying poisonous catfish. She flew around the world studying fish for over fifty years and became one of the world's leading ichthyologists. Her extensive research on sharks earned her the name, "Shark Lady."

Her American father managed a city pool in New York, where he met a young Japanese swimming instructor

"The Shark Lady," Eugenie Clark

whom he married. He and Yumiko taught Eugenie to swim at a young age, but Eugenie's father died when she was two. To reduce expenses, mother and daughter moved to Atlantic City, New Jersey, to live with Yumiko's parents. While Yumiko commuted daily to her job in Manhattan, Eugenie stayed with her grandparents. The nearby ocean offered all kinds of amusement for the young girl. Although she loved to explore the beach, her favorite thing to do was to jump in the ocean and open her eyes underwater to see what she could find on the sandy bottom.

In 1928 Yumiko and Eugenie moved to Queens, New York, where Eugenie started school when she was six. Skipping two grades and being the only Japanese-American in the school set her apart from her schoolmates. They often made fun of her, especially when she brought seaweed to eat at lunchtime. They thought it was carbon paper. Trying to shock them further, "I told them [my mother and I] ate rice with seaweed for breakfast, raw fish, octopus, and sea urchin eggs for supper, and cakes made from sharks."[2] Eugenie credited these early school experiences as character building.

Eugenie spent Saturdays at the New York Aquarium while her mother worked at the nearby Downtown Athletic Club. She never tired of watching sharks and loved to pretend that she was swimming with them. When homeless people came to the aquarium to escape bad weather, Eugenie talked to them about her observations of different fish. Her mother gave her an aquarium so that she could enjoy watching smaller fish at home. Soon almost every room had a fish tank. Eugenie kept a journal and began to teach herself all about fish. She watched them, drew them, and dissected them when they died.

At sixteen, Eugenie entered Hunter College in New York City. She qualified for free tuition because she was a state resident and she had high grades. She graduated from Hunter in 1942 with a degree in zoology, an unusual major for women in the

1940s. She wanted to learn about ichthyology, the study of fish, at Columbia University but the department chairman discouraged her. She could enroll, he said, but it would be a waste of time and money since she would probably choose to raise a family over having a career. Although she was married several times and had four children, she did not forego a career. She received her master's degree in 1946 from New York University and remained there to begin working toward her doctorate degree. Her professor, Dr. Charles M. Breder, encouraged her to study blowfish, specifically how they puffed themselves up. He was so impressed with her research that he asked if he might include it in a paper he was publishing. Eugenie could not believe that she would have her name included in a scientific research paper next to one of the world's leading ichthyologists.

Before she finished her doctoral dissertation, a well-known fish expert, Carl L. Hubbs, invited her to become a research assistant at the Scripps Institution of Oceanography in California. She studied "swell sharks" to see why they puffed up, and other sharks did not—a study very close to the one she had done under Dr. Breder. She learned to use a face mask and took her first deep-sea dive wearing a helmet. Wearing helmets allowed divers to remain underwater longer because the helmet connected to an oxygen pump in the boat above. Although Eugenie made several helmet dives, she did not go on overnight research trips because in 1946 people frowned upon a woman sleeping in the same quarters as men. She resented this restriction.

In 1949 she applied for a government grant to study poisonous fish in the Pacific Ocean. Afraid that she would be refused because she was a woman, Eugenie was delighted when her application was accepted. She spent the summer traveling between remote islands of Micronesia, completely enthralled with her surroundings both above sea level and below. On her dives she found a beautiful world of fish she had never seen before.

Although some fishermen were skeptical about the young female diver, she quickly endeared herself to them. She dove with an expert fisher on Guam who was so pleased when she ate his freshly caught squid that he promptly made her an honored guest of the island. Some of the local people willingly guided fish to tidal pools where they were poisoned. This method enabled Eugenie to carefully examine and make detailed drawings of each species as part of her research.

Eugenie then went to the Republic of Palau, a nation of small islands in the Pacific. The islands, really elevated coral reefs, were a home to a variety of sea life. Her guide was a skilled fisherman named Siakong. He showed Eugenie how to make spears out of bamboo and metal, and after many dives she mastered spearing triggerfish. Once Siakong was swimming along the bottom of a reef and Eugenie lowered herself to see what he was looking at. As she descended, she rested her hand on what she thought was a piece of coral. Siakong quickly grabbed her hand, realizing that it was resting on a giant clam at least four feet wide. These large clams got their food by clamping their shells so tightly that it was impossible to escape. Eugenie learned to tell the difference between coral and clams very quickly. On another island, since she was traveling alone, the island chief gave her a chaperone—a man—and they slept in a men's club. By the time she went home, she had collected, preserved, and cataloged many of the fish species that lived in the Pacific Ocean.

In 1950 she applied for a Fulbright Scholarship to further study poisonous fish in the Red Sea. Women in Egypt followed a strict dress code that allowed them to expose only their faces. Imagine how shocked they must have been to see Eugenie dressed for dives in two-piece bathing suits. She preferred diving around the Ras Muhammad peninsula, located at the southern end of the Sinai Desert. Eugenie found it to be a habitat for numerous types of fish, many similar to those she found in the Pacific Ocean. Students from nearby Faud University willingly helped her lure "blow heads," another type of fish that puffed up, into shallow pools of water where she could study them. She sent her findings to a medical research lab in California. As a result of her many hours underwater, she collected over 300 types of fish, three of which had never before been identified. "The Red Sea is blue,"[3] she loved to tell people, and it became one of her favorite places to dive.

In 1952 Eugenie accepted a job at Hunter College to teach biology. She gave birth to a daughter, Hera, but motherhood did not stop her career, as the Columbia professor had feared years earlier. In addition, she became a research associate at the American Museum of Natural History. While she submitted scientific papers to academic journals, she also wrote pieces for the recreational reader and in 1953 she wrote her first book, *Lady with a Spear*. The book became a best seller and there were many articles about the young diver in newspapers and magazines.

The book's popular success prompted Anne and Alfred Vanderbilt to invite Eugenie to address a group in Englewood, Florida, the following year. People flocked to hear the marine biologist. The Vanderbilts were so impressed that before Eugenie left, they asked her to set up a laboratory on their property in Florida and be its director. Now expecting her second child, Eugenie and her family moved south and she established the Cape Haze Marine Laboratory whose purpose was to collect and study marine life in the Gulf of Mexico. Soon her mother and stepfather joined them and opened a Japanese restaurant nearby.

The laboratory was a small building on a dock where Alfred Vanderbilt kept a 21-foot-long Chris Craft. Shortly after Eugenie arrived, the New England Institute of Medical Research requested a fresh shark liver for cancer research. Eugenie had never hunted sharks but Beryl Chadwick, who also worked at the laboratory, promptly baited traps with hooks of mullet. The sharks took the bait and suddenly the Vanderbilts' new employees were studying sharks. Eugenie wrote up the studies and the Cape Haze Laboratory made news. No one had ever studied sharks before and students from all over the world asked to come and volunteer. This encouraged Eugenie to apply for grants from the National Science Foundation and these funds allowed many young people to conduct research at the laboratory.

In 1956 she had her third child, Themistokles Alexander Konstantinu. Looking for a shorter name, Eugenie and her husband followed a friend's suggestion and called him by his initials, Tak. At about the same time, Eugenie discovered a fish called the sand bass. This species was unusual because it could be either sex, and it changed its colors accordingly. In 1958, expecting yet another child, Eugenie began to study learning behavior in sharks. Experimenting with lemon sharks, she and her assistants discovered that they could be taught to recognize shapes and colors and to press a bell when they were hungry. These experiments proved that sharks were intelligent.

In 1964 *National Geographic* sent Eugenie to the Red Sea to learn about garden eels. She was happy to return to one of her favorite diving areas and to share the experience with her children. Garden eels were difficult to study because they did not venture far from their burrows in the sand and retreated into them whenever they needed protection. Looking through face masks, the children watched as their mother dove to the bottom and tried to catch an eel. Hera sighted one just as her mother had given up luring it out. She screamed with excitement and Eugenie quickly dove to the bottom and grabbed the sought after eel. She had caught the first garden eel ever captured in Elat, Israel. A few days later, Nicholas, her fourth child, dove with her when she discovered a fish she'd never seen before. She caught it and put it in her son's face mask to keep it alive until they got it to the lab. Since she was the first person to describe the unknown fish, she was able to name it. In honor of her helper, Eugenie called the fish Trichonotus nikii.

Lady with a Spear was translated and published in Japan in 1965. The Crown Prince, who had a keen interest in marine biology, invited Eugenie to visit his country. He was eager to meet the woman who was the subject of so many published articles. As a gift for the leader of her mother's country, Eugenie brought him a trained nurse shark. She placed it in a small pool near the palace and Prince Akihito was amazed at the shark's response to Eugenie's commands. Eugenie and the Prince became friends and took many dives together.

Her career flourished and *Who's Who in America* named her one of fourteen outstanding women in the United States. In 1967 Eugenie decided to leave Florida and return to New York to teach. She suggested Perry Gilbert as her successor. Perry had gone on many dives with Eugenie and agreed with her philosophy that the lab should continue to focus on research and education. About that time, William Mote, a local businessman, approached Perry about expanding the laboratory. They bought land in Sarasota, Florida, built the new facility, and renamed it the Mote Marine Laboratory. For the next two years, Eugenie was an adviser and trustee of the laboratory as well as a visiting professor at the New England Institute for Medical Research.

Committed to teaching, in 1968 she accepted an offer from the University of Maryland at College Park to join its Zoology Department, where she remained for twenty-four years. Students loved her lectures and the spectacular films she brought with her from her latest dives. During this time she also conducted research in over twenty countries. She returned to the Red Sea in 1973 to learn more about the fish, Moses sole, which protected itself from predators by secreting a substance that repelled sharks. Eugenie collected the milky liquid, put it on various objects, and lowered them into the water. Sharks would come close but immediately turned away from anything containing the acidic liquid. Hoping that the spray might prevent shark attacks on humans, scientists tried to duplicate it, but found that synthetic sprays were too costly and were unstable.

Readers learned about habits of deep-sea creatures through articles that Eugenie wrote for *National Geographic* magazine. Of special interest was her article about sleeping sharks. People believed that sharks had to move to keep alive, but on her many dives in Mexican waters, Eugenie found several sleeping sharks in caves far below the water's surface. Perhaps it was not sleep as humans know it, she reported, but the sharks seemed to be very still and tranquil. *National Geographic* photographed her for its April 1975 cover in an underwater cave with a sleeping shark.

When asked what her favorite sharks were, Eugenie said there were two. The first was the lemon shark that she trained in the early days at the Cape Haze Marine Laboratory. The second was the whale shark because it was the largest fish in the sea. On a dive in Baja, a whale shark swam by her. Without thinking she grabbed onto its dorsal fin, which she said was the size of a large piano. She was not afraid because the shark did not dive deep. She held on for about twenty or thirty yards before she realized that her oxygen might give out. "But I was so sorry to let go of the most beautiful ride of my life,"[4] she later said.

Eugenie retired from the University of Maryland in 1992. She continued to lecture, write, and dive. In 1998, while diving in New Guinea, she found a fish she'd never seen before. It had black stripes similar to an old prison uniform, which led Eugenie to name it the convict fish. It was a new riddle for her. Because the fish never left its cave, it was not clear how it ate or gave birth. Videotaping its behavior did not answer her questions. Further observation led her to believe that the young left the caves to gather food for the adults. In 2007, at age eighty-five, Eugenie returned to New Guinea to continue her study of the species.

Eugenie frequently lectured on the declining health of the ocean and its inhabitants. She expressed concern over the decreasing population of sharks because of over-fishing. She told her audiences that for the most part sharks do not attack people—that people are more dangerous to sharks because they catch the fish to use in shark fin soup and other delicacies. She worried about pollution and was determined to educate her audience about the results of over-development. Building near shorelines destroyed natural habitats for marine life. Coral reefs have disappeared. She was pleased that she was influential in making Egypt's underground park, Ras Muhammad, its first national park.

Eugenie was a pioneer in underwater exploration. Over the years she had support from others in her field and earned their respect and admiration. She was the recipient of many awards, produced television programs, and wrote books and numerous articles. She discovered new species of fish and had three named for her. She had underwater experiences that most people can't begin to imagine. Some have said that Eugenie Clark never lost her childhood fascination with fish. She passed the wonder of underwater exploration on to her students and to those who had the privilege to work with her.

Lucille Clifton, 1936-2010
Poet

Lucille Clifton was born Thelma Louise Sayles in Depew, New York, into one of the only black families in town. She had two half sisters, Josie, who was several years older than Lucille, and Elaine, who was closer to her in age and would become her close companion for many years. When Lucille was two years old the family welcomed the birth of a baby boy, Sammy, who was called "Hon." Neither of their parents, Samuel and Thelma Moore Sayles, had graduated from high school. Samuel worked in the local steel mill and Thelma was a homemaker. But their youngest daughter would become a celebrated author, would win some of the most prestigious literary prizes in the world, would be a college professor though she did not have a college degree, and would be awarded several honorary doctorates.

Lucille was unusual right from the start because, like her mother before her, she was born with twelve fingers, six on each hand. The doctor removed the extra digits. In Depew the Sayles family lived on Muskingum Street at the top of a hill, and from her house young Lucille could see her Grandmother Moore's house and the goat she kept in her backyard. Samuel took pride that his was the first black family in town to have a full dining room set, which he bought in Buffalo on credit. Lucille remembered that a man from People's store would come to the house each Saturday to collect the weekly payment.

When she was still very young the family moved to Buffalo, where there was a larger black community. Lucille recalled that everyone loved her mother, and Thelma's love for her family was limitless. She was her daughter's protector. Once, when five-year-old Lucille was to recite a piece during a Christmas program, the child froze, forgot her lines, and could not speak. Her mother swooped down the aisle to the little girl, declaring loudly that her daughter did not have to do anything she didn't want to. Her baby was safe in her arms. Thelma, an epileptic, was in fragile health and would die when Lucille was in her early twenties, but her influence and her story would live on in her daughter. Thelma wrote poetry using iambic pentameter, and gently criticized Lucille, whose early attempts at poems were not limited by that structure, rhythm, and rhyme. Thelma's marriage to Samuel Sayles was a bit one-sided; she was faithful while he was not. She was an obedient wife and when her husband insisted that no wife of his would write poetry for publication, she followed his orders and burned her work. Yet she would later urge Lucille to get away and have a better life, not a life like hers.

Her father gave Lucille and her brother and sisters a sense of words and their power. He brought them examples of rich language, reading them the poems of Langston Hughes and Paul Laurence Dunbar, and telling them ghost stories he made up himself. Yet he never learned to write, he drank too much, and he abused his youngest daughter.

However, her mother and father gave her a gift: they were great newspaper readers and were curious about what they read. Lucille inherited their curiosity about the world and thrived on it. She was a writer even as a young girl. She made up stories to tell her sisters and brother and led them to play games full of imagination. At night, when Elaine was uneasy because she could hear mice in the dresser drawer, younger sister Lucille would sing to her to block out the noise. The two girls had respect and affection for each other and they, along with their mother, enjoyed and spoiled Hon.

Her Grandmother Moore nicknamed her "Genius." Lucille was a fine student in school and her grades were excellent. She continued to write both for her classes and on her own, and when she graduated from high school at age sixteen she won a scholarship to the prestigious black college, Howard University, in Washington, DC. She was the first person from her Baptist church to go off to college and it was an exciting time. But Howard, which some people confused with Harvard, would not be at all like home and friends warned her about staying away from certain areas of Washington.

A nervous Lucille traveled to the city with her friends Retha and Betty. While she was a large young woman, many of her female classmates were lighter-skinned and had lighter bodies as well. When the girls got off the train they were met by a young man from Howard who cheerfully welcomed the chic and attractive Betty, then turned to Lucille and politely asked if she was Betty's mother. Right away she felt awkward and out of place. Her family's lack of money set her apart, too. Her clothes were not at all stylish and she kept her trunk, borrowed from her grandmother and tied together with a rope, in the dormitory's basement, sneaking downstairs to get a change of clothes when she needed to. There were several fascinating people on campus but Lucille did not yet have the confidence to meet them as equals. She lasted a year at Howard then fled home, her scholarship lost to poor grades.

Willing to try college again, but nearer to Buffalo, Lucille enrolled at Fredonia State Teachers College. That did not work either. It seemed her need to learn and the college's need to teach did not connect. Her father was angry and disappointed. However, she continued to write, and through friends she met Fred Clifton, a student at the University of Buffalo. She and Fred married in 1958. He worked toward a Ph.D. in philosophy at the university and Lucille found a job as a clerk in the state's unemployment office. The following year brought sadness to the family. Thelma Sayles died of epilepsy at age forty-four. Just a month after her death, Lucille and Fred's first child, daughter Sidney, was born. Like her mother and grandmother, the baby had twelve fingers, and like the doctors before, this doctor removed the two extra digits. By 1965 Lucille and Fred had six children and Lucille carried on her family's tradition of telling them stories.

In 1969 the Clifton family was living in Baltimore, where Fred worked as the education coordinator for the Model Cities program and Lucille worked at the US Office of Education. She continued to write poems while working and tending to her family. She sent some of the poems to poet Robert Hayden, hoping he could help her find a way to find a publisher for them. He shared them with another poet, Carolyn Kizer. She was impressed with them and entered them in the 1969 YM/YWCA Poetry Center contest. Lucille won the contest; the Discovery Award was the first of many prizes and awards she would win for writing.

And she had more good news that year. Random House published her first book of poems, *Good Times*, in November, and the *New York Times* chose it as one of the best books of the year. November was also the month the Holt company published her first picture book for children, *Some of the Days of Everett Anderson*. It would become the first in a series of Everett Anderson books focusing on a young black boy and his family. Most children's books published in the United States then were about white children and white families. Lucille Clifton insisted both children and adults needed windows and mirrors—windows to see outside oneself, mirrors to see oneself. There were very few mirrors for children who were not white. Only rarely could they pick up a book and see themselves. Conversely, white youngsters were at a disadvantage as well because they had so many mirrors, yet very few windows that opened onto things and people who were not like them. The Everett Anderson books would help create a better balance. Beginning with the 1969 publication of *Some of the Days of Everett Anderson,* the Everett Anderson books became popular. In 1984 *Everett Anderson's Goodbye* was published. In that book young Everett's father dies, and the boy experiences the five stages of grief: denial, anger, bargaining, depression, and finally acceptance. The book was an instant classic and Lucille received the Coretta Scott King Award. Other books in the series include *Everett Anderson's 1,2,3*; which deals with the possibility that his mother may remarry; *One of the Problems of Everett Anderson,* in which a friend is physically abused; and *Everett Anderson's Nine Month Long*, which ends with the birth of his sister. There were many windows, and many mirrors, in these books.

Although 1969 was an exciting year for the Clifton family, it brought sadness as well as joy. Lucille's father, Samuel Sayles, had a heart attack and died. He was sixty-seven years old. His storytelling, love of reading, and his ambitions for his daughter were strong positive influences on her, yet he abused and hurt her as well, and as an adult she struggled with their complex relationship. Ultimately she would dedicate a book to him.

In 1970 editors Langston Hughes and Arna Bontemps, chose Lucille's work to be included in *Poetry of the Negro 1746-1970.* Her second book, *Good News about the Earth*, was published in 1972 and was followed by *An Ordinary Woman* in 1974. That same year Coppin State College in Baltimore named her Poet in Residence and from 1975 to 1985 she served as Poet Laureate in Maryland. More books of poetry for adults followed, and in 1976 she received an Emmy for her work on the screenplay for the television program *Free to Be You and Me.* In 1980 her book *Two-Headed Woman* won the Juniper Prize sponsored by the University of Massachusetts Press; it was also nominated for a Pulitzer Prize

In 1984 Lucille suffered a great loss when Fred Clifton died of cancer. He was just forty-nine years old and they had been married for more than twenty-six years. Lucille needed a change and spent the next several years at the University of California at Santa Cruz. During that time she published two books, *Next* and *Good Woman: Poems and a Memoir*; both books were finalists for the Pulitzer Prize in 1988. In an interview with poet Carolyn Kizer, Lucille noted that she liked the Pacific Ocean. Unlike the Atlantic, it was not a slavery road for her people.

In 1989 she returned to Maryland when St. Mary's College named her a Visiting Distinguished Professor of Literature. PBS featured her in a documentary, *The Power of the Word,* and the New York Public Library named her a "Literary Lion." By 1991, though still at St. Mary's, her title changed: she was now a Distinguished Professor of Humanities at the college, and she published another book of poetry, *Quilting*, which was nominated for a Pulitzer Prize.

She was named a Maryland Living Treasure in 1993, the same year Loyola College awarded her the Andrew White Medal. During that time she also taught at Columbia University in New York City. More honors and awards followed throughout the decade. Poor health, though, dogged her during the mid-nineties. She was diagnosed with breast cancer and underwent a lumpectomy. When she suffered kidney failure in 1997, her youngest daughter, Alexia, donated a kidney to save her mother's life. The

Terrible Stories, published in 1998, reflected the weariness of the aging body. More sadness followed in the next few years. Her daughter Fredrica died of a brain tumor in 2000 and four years later her son Channing died of heart failure.

Yet the awards and honors increased. She spent a year at Duke University as a Distinguished Visiting Professor, and then held the Hilda Landers Chair at St. Mary's College. She was named a fellow of the American Academy of Arts and Sciences and was elected to the Board of Chancellors of the Academy of American Poets. Though she had not been able to come to terms with the academics at Howard University in 1954, she was inducted into Phi Beta Kappa in 1998. A new book, *Blessing the Boats*, was published in 2000, and it was chosen the winner of the National Book Award. In 2007 she was awarded the Ruth Lilly Poetry Prize, given by the Poetry Foundation in honor of the lifetime accomplishments of a US poet. It included a cash award of $100,000.

Lucille Clifton's journey was unusual. She was a child of an unequal marriage, with a mother who personified love, yet was limited by her shyness and her epilepsy, and a father whose hopes for his daughter were high, yet whose behavior was so hurtful that the hurt could not be repaired. She was driven and curious to learn, yet she and the colleges she attended could not find a place where they could teach and she could learn. She was a black woman poet at a time when the Civil Rights and Feminist movements were on the front page of every newspaper, yet her poems, while some expressed anger, were not militant or belligerent in their tone. They were intensely personal and reflected her family and her experiences. Some of them were joyful and playful. Others addressed the saddest and most troubling aspects of her life. As she examined those particular things with great care, readers could begin to make connections to their own lives. Her tenderness, energy, and insight encouraged her audience to discover a balance between opposites and to find both mirrors and windows.

The little girl in Buffalo who entertained her siblings with stories and soothed her nervous sister with singing found a vast family to entertain, to teach, and to soothe.

The Cone Sisters
Etta Cone,
1870-1949
Claribel Cone,
1864-1929

Claribel Cone, Gertrude Stein, and Etta Cone, 1903

Art Collectors

How was it that Claribel and Etta Cone had the courage to buy what would become an outstanding collection of modern art—one that would document the post World War I art world? What led them to buy paintings and prints that most people considered scandalous? It certainly wasn't their background. They grew up during the Victorian era and followed its rules of dress and decorum. Their father, Herman Kahn, was a Jewish immigrant from Bavaria. When he came to America, he met and married Helen Guggenheimer in Richmond, Virginia. Although they changed their name to Cone, they felt unwelcome and moved to Tennessee. But anti-Semitism existed there, too, and furthermore, jobs were scarce. The Cones moved again, this time to Baltimore, Maryland. After the Civil War, many people came to this city, whose port and railroad provided jobs. Baltimore also had a large German Jewish population. Feeling comfortable in this environment, Herman and his family settled in. He and his two oldest sons opened a wholesale grocery store on the waterfront.

The Cone family prospered in Baltimore. They lived on Eutaw Place, a fashionable city address in the 1870s. Their thirteen children lived a carefree childhood, had many friends, and received an excellent education. Claribel and Etta graduated from Western Female High School. They were sisters with totally different interests and personalities—Etta enjoyed music, Claribel liked books and preferred her own company. Claribel was large in stature, handsome, and quite sure of herself. She enjoyed science and became a doctor, graduating from the Woman's Medical College of Baltimore in 1890. Marriage and maintaining a household were not for her. Typical of her personality, she signed all letters, Dr. Claribel Cone. Most women doctors at the time placed an M.D. after their name, but Claribel wanted to make sure that people knew she was a doctor. Etta, even taller than her sister, had the same dark hair and strong features. In awe of her older sister Claribel, Etta was shy and timid. She was much happier staying home and playing the piano.

Claribel continued her medical studies in Philadelphia and two years later was accepted into a residency program there at the Blockley Hospital. She was one of two women to receive an offer. But when she found the staff condescending to women, she returned to Baltimore and furthered her medical education at the Johns Hopkins Medical School, which had opened its doors to women in 1893.

During these years the sisters met Leo and Gertrude Stein, who were to have a great influence on their lives and on their art education. The four were introduced when Leo and Gertrude came to live with their Baltimore aunt, Fannie Bachrach, a neighbor of the Cones. When Claribel invited them to join her Saturday evening gatherings, her guests were astounded by the Steins' outrageous behavior and attire. Gertrude was large, quite outspoken, and she chose to ignore Victorian etiquette. She did not wear corsets and thought nothing of propping her feet on tables. Her brother, Leo, well dressed, and somewhat of a flirt with women, would talk a great deal about art and music. While Gertrude and Claribel would dominate most of the conversation in loud voices and hearty laughter, it was Leo and his discussions of art that fascinated Etta. But the Steins would soon move to Boston, Leo first to Harvard and then Gertrude enrolled in what became Radcliffe College.

After Herman Cone died, his oldest son, Moses, gave Etta $300 to buy something cheery for their home. Rather than buying a piece of furniture, she went to New York and hired a bidder to buy as many Theodore Robinson paintings as her money would allow. She was able to get five. Her family was horrified and stunned by an independence that was uncharacteristic of Etta. At a time when most families had simple reproductions of religious art or landscapes that cost fifteen dollars or less, these paintings were of the ultra-modern impressionist school and they were expensive. This was a style of painting where the artist creates images using different brush strokes to duplicate color and shifting light. No one knew how she heard about Theodore Robinson's estate sale, but these five paintings would become the core for The Cone Collection.

Realizing that it was unlikely that either of the sisters would marry, in 1901, their brothers gave each of them an annual allowance of $2400 as part of the family inheritance. This financial cushion made it possible for Etta to travel. She felt stifled by life on Eutaw Place and was fascinated by Gertrude's stories of her summer visits with Leo, who was studying art in Europe. She wanted to go abroad and experience life beyond Baltimore. Since Claribel was busy with medical studies, Etta sailed to Europe with a cousin and a friend in the spring of that year. This was the first of thirty-two trips that one or both sisters would take to the continent during their lifetime.

Leo met the ship in Naples and guided the three women through Italy. In Florence they spent many hours at the Uffizi Gallery, where he introduced them to Renaissance art. When looking at art, he told Etta to think about how the painting made her feel, but this was hard for her. She'd rather hear the story describing the painting; it would take some time before she could look at and appreciate paint strokes.

The three women visited Cone relatives in Germany, but Etta found that country dark and cold. She was much happier when they arrived in Paris, which she found sunny and bright. There the group met Leo and Gertrude, who was on another of her summer visits. The Louvre became a magnet to Etta and she spent many hours walking through its rooms, studying and absorbing everything she saw. The Steins developed an interest in Japanese prints and encouraged Etta to buy some, which she did. When she returned to Baltimore in October she was already planning her next trip.

That trip would be postponed because of family responsibilities. Her mother was ill and it was not until after her death in 1903 that Etta returned to Europe. This time Claribel and another cousin joined her. Claribel took a leave of absence from the Women's Medical College of Baltimore, where she was now a member of the faculty. She planned to tour the continent before going to Germany to conduct research at the

Senckenberg Institute. Once again, the ship docked in Naples and for the first time the sisters reversed roles. Etta was in charge. Following the itinerary of her earlier trip, she led the women first to Florence. After visiting the Uffizzi Gallery, Etta wrote in her diary that her understanding of art was growing. The ladies went on to Frankfurt and after spending a summer there they traveled to Paris and met the Steins. After a short visit, Claribel returned to the Institute and Etta to Baltimore.

When Etta went to Europe in 1904, she stayed for three years. First she visited Claribel in Germany and then they both went to Paris. They were happy to see Gertrude and Leo and to meet the Steins' brother, Michael, and his wife, Sally. The six friends spent many hours visiting galleries. Leo was now collecting paintings by four artists whom he felt were leading art in a new direction, Renoir, Degas, Cezanne, and Manet. The sisters were shocked by what they saw.

People recognized that Leo was a serious collector and one who knew a great deal about twentieth century painting. At the 1905 Paris Autumn Salon, there was a special room for new artists, including a group who were going beyond impressionism by painting abstract figures with bold colors. Parisians did not like their art and the critics were unmerciful in their reviews, calling them *Les Fauves*, or "the Wild Beasts." Leo added to the furor when he bought *La Femme au Chapeau* from Henri Matisse, who was considered to be the leader of *Les Fauves*. He paid Matisse $100 for the painting. Although Leo and his cousins purchased more paintings from Matisse, Etta was not ready to buy any of the artist's works—yet.

Claribel returned to her beloved Germany and Etta rented an apartment in Paris near her friends. She loved being in the art world and was fascinated by its bohemian atmosphere. She began visiting artists in their studios and two of them, Pablo Picasso and Henri Matisse, would become good friends. At this time Picasso was painting Gertrude's portrait and Etta went with her to one of the sittings. The studio was filthy and filled with broken furniture and unwashed dishes. Etta paid no attention and looked carefully at the drawings strewn around the studio. With her growing understanding of art, she was impressed by the artist's techniques and bought two of his drawings that afternoon. She would eventually own 113 Picassos.

A few months later Sally Stein took her to meet Matisse. Etta was happily surprised to enter a tidy apartment and meet a neatly dressed man. She could not believe that this polite man was the leader of the "Wild Beasts." She knew art critics made fun of his paintings, but when Matisse explained how he painted, Etta changed her mind about his work. On that visit, she bought two drawings. She soon became a patron of Matisse, as well as other struggling artists. But Matisse remained her favorite and she bought many of his paintings over the years.

When Claribel visited her sister in Paris in the spring of 1906, she was startled by the paintings that she found in her sister's Paris apartment and she was surprised at Etta's frequent visits to see her artist friends in Montmartre. But she did go with her sister for another of Gertrude's portrait sittings—this visit to Picasso's studio may have been the beginning of Claribel's interest in art. She could not speak French nor could Picasso speak English, but they both had lasting impressions of that first meeting. Claribel considered him more a boy than an upcoming artist. Picasso thought this regal woman looked like an empress and always referred to her as such. Before they left Picasso's studio, the sisters bought several pieces of his art for twenty or thirty dollars.

In 1907 the sisters joined their brother Moses and his family for a trip around the world. Very often the group disagreed on which sites they'd like to see. Claribel could be stubborn and tardy which irritated Moses. When they sailed the Nile River in Egypt, Claribel captured the interest of a sultan who asked Moses if he could buy her. Moses refused the offer. Fortunately they all had a common fondness—shopping. The two sisters purchased lace, jewels, silks, and carpets that would become part of the vast Cone collection. If they found something they liked, they bought it in multiples.

Letters from home saying that Moses was seriously ill interrupted their 1908 European excursion. When Moses died in December, Etta was especially grief-stricken and suffered from a recurring stomach problem. The Women's Medical College in Baltimore had closed its doors, leaving Claribel without a place to work. Feeling adrift, she returned to Germany where she immersed herself in opera and other cultural events that Munich offered. She wrote Etta, who remained in North Carolina to be with Moses' wife, "Oh, how I love this random wandering…I have not been so happy for a long time as I am now…I realize that I am not happy in America."[1]

When Etta met her sister in Paris in 1912 they found many changes. The Steins were arguing among themselves and no longer held Saturday salons. Leo did not like the new Cubist movement, an art form that used geometrical shapes as images. When Picasso began painting in Cubist style, Leo no longer spoke to him. The sisters' artist friends were now prosperous and had moved away from Montmartre. People were buying their art and no longer considered them "the Wild Beasts." The sisters returned to Baltimore at the end of the year and Etta rented an apartment next to Claribel's in the Marlborough building on Eutaw Street—not far from where they grew up.

Before they took their annual trip the following year, Claribel told her sister that she would stay in Germany and would not be returning to Baltimore. She was living in Munich when World War I broke out in 1914. She moved into a luxurious suite at the Regina Palast Hotel and typically did her best to ignore the war, by continuing her habits of rising late, exercising, visiting relatives, and making countless lists in countless notebooks. She enjoyed being the topic of conversation among the hotel guests who wondered whom this stately formidable woman was who was traveling alone. Later she wrote an ecstatic letter to Etta that King Ludwig mistook her for royalty.

She refused to return to the United States even when her brother, Caesar, made arrangements for her. As the war went on, things became worse. Mail was stopped between Germany and the United States. Claribel's bank account was frozen and she had to borrow money from relatives. Although she was concerned when soldiers searched her hotel rooms, she was cordial and after she offered them hot chocolate they left. She remained in Munich for seven years. In 1919 the German nationalist movement began holding secret meetings. Newspapers wrote articles about the movement's new leader, Adolf Hitler, and his anti-Semitic statements. Finally Claribel returned home.

The Cone family business prospered from the war, making the sisters quite wealthy. When they were ready to travel again, they went to Paris in the summer of 1922, and they went on a huge shopping spree, buying from art galleries and from artists. Picasso offered to paint Claribel's portrait and before they went home they packed numerous crates containing pieces of sculpture, lithographs, and paintings mostly by Matisse and Picasso. They bought more the following summer. In 1925 Claribel bought Cezanne's painting, *Mont Sainte-Victoire*, for $18,800. Neither sister would spend that much on one painting again. Each differed from the other in what she liked. Etta preferred paintings of flowers, landscapes, and nature—subjects that were still proper for Victorian society. Claribel chose more avant-garde works whose subjects were large and painted with bold strokes. Claribel's thoughts on purchasing art were clear in a letter she wrote to Etta when her sister was hesitant about buying a painting. "I should say if it's pretty (as you say it is) attractive, and it is decorative and pleases you—who cares a darn what anyone else says…"[2]

For several years the sisters continued this pattern of summer European shopping trips and they spent the winters arranging their new acquisitions in their Baltimore apartments. Stacked paintings, piles of notebooks, and large pieces of furniture made Claribel's apartment too crowded for comfortable living. As a result, she rented another apartment on the same floor. Now she had a place to live and a place to keep her growing collection. The sisters did not buy things with the intent of building a collection; they bought them to provide beauty in their surroundings just as Etta had done in 1898 when she bought the Robinson paintings. Claribel wrote, "As a matter of fact…I didn't even know that the things I had could be a collection…Ever since I was small girl and picked up all the shells I could find, reveling in their color and in their forms, I've been acquiring beautiful things."[3] A nephew recalled that his aunts either wore their possessions or hung them on the walls of every room, including the bathroom. When greeting guests, the sisters enhanced their Victorian clothing with new jewelry, shawls, and lace.

But they were growing older and becoming concerned about the future of everything that they had accumulated. Many museums expressed an interest in buying what was now considered a collection. Although Baltimore was home, the city was still provincial in its artistic tastes. When the Baltimore Museum of Art (BMA) first opened, Etta offered to loan it some of her paintings. The museum's curators did not want them. Claribel had written in her will that the BMA would be the beneficiary only if Etta felt that people in Baltimore could appreciate modern art. After Claribel's death on September 29, 1929, the city newspapers worked hard to emphasize the importance of the collection. The museum's officials spent many hours convincing Etta the art collection belonged in Baltimore.

When Matisse came to America on business in 1930, he took time to see Etta in Baltimore. For the first time he was able to see how carefully the sisters had arranged his works and he was impressed by the size of their collection. Each year after that visit, Matisse saved two or three of his works for Etta to see, helping her to make a final decision. *The Baltimore Sun* wrote a story about his visit, and as a result, the art world now recognized Etta as a major collector.

Etta continued her annual journeys abroad, often taking nieces and nephews with her. One nephew, Harold, recalled that Etta followed the same regimen each day beginning with a breakfast meeting where the group would decide the day's activities. If Etta did not want to go, she complained of a stomachache and remained at the hotel. He remembered that despite his aunt having a different purse for each day and numerous pockets that had been made for her petticoats in which to store valuables, she still lost things. He loved to tell his children that when the group returned to their rooms in the evening, it was his duty to "make the strange men check." Fearful that someone might be hiding under the bed or in a closet, Harold Cone checked the hotel rooms to appease his Aunt Etta.

On one of Etta's last trips Matisse invited her to his studio. He appreciated the support he had received over the years from his "two Baltimore ladies" and he told Etta that he had a special surprise. When she arrived at his apartment, she saw that he had recreated a real life scene from the painting, *Le Robe Tilleul*, which she had bought the year before. There sat the young lady, dressed in yellow, in front of an open window and shutter. Etta was delighted. At the same time she commissioned Matisse to draw a portrait of Claribel. Sketching from memory and photographs, he presented the drawings to Etta—four of Claribel and six of Etta. It took him three years. He later wrote to a friend describing this experience as difficult because he was drawing two people in the same family who were complete opposites.

As a tribute to Claribel, Etta, with the help her of her Swiss cousin, Siegried, began to catalogue the collection. Nothing would be left out. She wanted each item shown on its own single page with its history on the opposite page. It also included small drawings and sketches that later were included in larger pieces of art. She felt that this would help art students understand the creative work of a particular artist. When the catalogue was completed, Etta sent copies to friends and to museums. She was pleased with the response she received because she felt the work gave meaning to the collection, something of lasting value. But it was not to be. The book was printed in Nazi-occupied Germany and when Etta realized this, she had the plates destroyed.

World War II stopped her summer trips to Europe, and during those years she bought what art she could from New York art dealers. In the early war years, she spent her time showing her collection to visitors in her apartment. The who's who in the art world came to Baltimore; they were amazed at the depth of the collection, especially by the number of paintings by Matisse that showed his evolving style through the decades.

As the war continued on and family members and friends died, Etta stopped having visitors. She wanted time alone to reflect on all that she and Claribel had amassed. Since Claribel's death twenty years earlier, Etta felt that Baltimore had matured in its view of modern art. In 1949 she made her decision and wrote in her will that the Baltimore Museum of Art would receive the 3,000-piece collection and an additional $400,000 to build a wing in which to display it. She died on August 30, 1949. The Cone Collection that Claribel and Etta spent a lifetime assembling is unique in the art world and an integral and permanent part of the Baltimore Museum of Art

Virginia Hall, 1906-1982
World War II Spy

Virginia Hall grew up as part of a comfortable family in Baltimore, Maryland. Her father was a successful real estate investor who owned several movie theaters. By the time she graduated from Roland Park Country School in 1924, she had begun to show signs that she was not just a well-educated young woman on her way to college. Her keen intelligence, her determination, and her willingness to follow a different path set her apart. During World War II, while her friends and family were dealing with ration cards and blackout shades, Virginia was hunted throughout France by the Nazi Gestapo as one of the most dangerous and effective spies for the Allies.

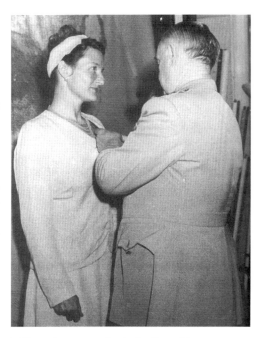

William Donovan, chief of Office of Strategic Services, awarding Virginia Hall with the Distinguished Service Cross, 1945.

The Halls had a house in the city, but they spent as much time as possible at Box Horn Farm, their 110-acre country home 20 miles away in rural Baltimore County. It was a working farm, complete with horses, cows, goats, and chickens. The large house did not have central heating, but its fireplaces and wood stoves kept the family comfortable. Its shelves were full of books, and it had both a tennis court and a kitchen garden nearby. Virginia thrived in the country. She rode horses and hunted birds and small animals on the farm, learned to catch and clean fish, and knew how to milk a cow. Her father taught her how to handle a gun when she was very young. It was a glorious place to grow up, and Virginia, a happy and confident tomboy, took advantage of everything Box Horn had to offer.

In 1912 she entered Roland Park Country School in the city. She enjoyed challenges and was a strong student with a special talent for languages. She excelled as an athlete, was chosen captain of both the varsity field hockey and basketball teams, and she was also an accomplished actress. Slender and 5 feet 7 inches tall, she was somewhat taller than average, and she often played the male lead roles in school productions. She was good at disguising her real identity and pretending to be someone else. Her classmates enjoyed and appreciated her, electing her class president in their senior year. They chose her as the "most original" among them, and noted that the one thing they expected from her was the unexpected. She was editor of her class yearbook, and on her senior page she described herself as "cantankerous and capricious." After graduating in 1924 she studied further at Radcliffe and Barnard Colleges, then looked for something more. Her search led her to the Sorbonne in Paris, where she studied at The Ecole des Services Politiques. The following year she was accepted at the Konsular Akademie in Vienna and graduated in 1929. She returned home to study French and economics at George Washington University, and she set her hopes on getting a job with the United States Foreign Service.

She first applied in 1929. The Civil Service exam was more difficult than she expected, and her scores were not strong enough. She kept hoping for a Foreign Service career but took a clerical job at the American Embassy in Warsaw, Poland, in 1931. Virginia applied again to the Foreign Service, still hoping to become a diplomat, and again arranged to take the exam. Mysteriously, while part of the test arrived in Warsaw, one section never appeared and so she was unable to complete the exam. In 1933 she transferred to Smyrna, Turkey. The climate there was comfortable and allowed her many different outdoor activities, and she was happy to go horseback riding and hunting once again. One day in December she arranged a hunting party for a few friends from the consulate and one of her Turkish neighbors. They shared a picnic lunch, and then set off to hunt snipe. Virginia carried a 12-gauge shotgun that had belonged to her father. As she climbed over a wire fence her foot slipped, and the gun caught on her coat and fired into her leg. Her friends applied a tourniquet to her leg and were able to slow the bleeding and get her to a hospital, which saved her life, but doctors were unable to mend her leg. They amputated it below the knee and Virginia went back to Maryland to recover. She was given an artificial leg, which she strapped to her thigh. It had a rubber sole to keep her from slipping. Virginia assumed that she could adapt to this new situation and that the prosthesis, like anything else, could be mastered with practice. With the help of a physiotherapist, she practiced walking with crutches, then with a cane, and finally walked on her own. In the fall of 1934, she asked to return to an embassy or consulate and she was assigned to a consulate in Venice, Italy.

It had beautiful furnishings, plenty of staff, and the atmosphere was relaxed and very social. Virginia was still a clerk, but sometimes she was allowed to fill in doing jobs that would normally be assigned to a Foreign Service officer. She applied again to take the Foreign Service exam, but, again, the questions for the oral section of the exam did not arrive. Then a letter came from the Assistant Secretary of State saying Virginia's amputation disqualified her from joining the Foreign Service. At the time there were 1500 Foreign Service officers. Six of them were women. It seemed to Virginia that women, especially those with opinions, were not wanted. She appealed the decision but was denied. Feeling unsettled, she transferred to Tallinn, Estonia, hoping the change would rekindle her interest in the Foreign Service. It did not, and Virginia resigned in 1939 and went to Paris.

Europe was changing. Adolph Hitler rose to power in Germany, as did Benito Mussolini in Italy. Many German, Austrian, and Czech Jews, fleeing danger at home, moved to the United States. Others crowded into Paris. The French disliked the newcomers and anti-Semitism grew rapidly. Virginia was disturbed by the rise of fascist leaders and angry that the United States did not seem to want to get involved in European problems. Then, on September 1, 1939, Hitler bombed Poland and World War II was underway. Virginia and a French friend volunteered as ambulance drivers, taking wounded French soldiers from the battlefront to field hospitals. As the German army advanced into France, their work became intense, with long hours and, for Virginia, pain from her stump. She continued to work as a driver until the next August. By that time France's government had surrendered and what was left of it moved from Paris to Vichy under the direction of Marshal Petain. Many Frenchmen were angry at their leaders' surrender and were ashamed that their country had given in so quickly. General Charles deGaulle called on his countrymen not to submit but to continue to fight. The French Resistance was born.

As Virginia traveled to Spain, where she would board a boat to go to London, she met an interesting man named George Bellows. They talked for a long time and found they thought very much alike. He introduced her to several friends and suggested that she contact friends of his in London and that she be sure to check in with the American Embassy there. When she arrived she went to the Embassy and was welcomed like a celebrity. People were anxious to hear what she had learned in France. She told them that the food shortage was a critical problem. She also said that, in her judgment, in spite of the fact the French government had given in, there were many French people who would be willing to rebel against the Nazis. When the Embassy offered her a job as a clerk she took it because she knew it might lead to more direct anti-Nazi work.

It did, but the opportunity she hoped for did not come from the American government. For some time the British government had developed an organization that specialized in secret operations. In the fall of 1940, through people she met after her talks with George Bellows, she was recruited to join that group, the British Special Operations Executive, the SOE. She resigned her job at the American Embassy. Along with other recruits, she was given thorough training in weapons, communications, resistance activities, and security. The training was physically and mentally demanding and many people could not meet the standards. Virginia could and did. Her outspokenness and directness were assets now. Waiting for her assignment was the most difficult task so far. Finally she was given a job. She would be Brigitte LeContre, an American citizen who spoke French fluently, and she would pose as a writer for a New York newspaper. Her real task would be to develop a spy network in Vichy, France.

She arrived in the town of Vichy in August 1941. At the American Embassy a clerk took her information and directed her to the Vichy government headquarters where she registered as a foreigner. Then she went to the hotel the SOE had suggested and rented a room that faced the street. She was in a good spot to see what was going on. Lack of food was on everyone's mind, and food was what Virginia wrote about in the first article she sent to her newspaper. Citizens were allowed to buy only very small amounts of meat, sugar, cheese, and some other things. The illegal black market, which sold rationed goods for many times their value, was active. Virginia also wrote a report, in code, for the SOE. In it she recorded what she had learned about the Vichy government and how she felt the local people would respond to resistance activities. She handed this report to a visiting SOE member in a sealed envelope and he took it to London.

Her next job was to go to Lyon, about two hours away by train. Again she registered as Brigitte LeContre, and again she rented a room that faced the street. She met an SOE contact, Dr. Jean Rousset, who would be a great help in her work. Then she began the difficult process of meeting people who volunteered to help the Resistance and deciding who to include in her network. The Nazis had spies who claimed to be pro-French but were actually working for the Germans and so she had to be careful. The Resistance fighters needed money, and Virginia had brought a supply of francs with her to Lyon. She was surprised and pleased that the resistance work she had been sent to do could begin immediately, and they were equally pleased to welcome her; her presence was a clear signal that the British were ready to help. Among Dr. Rousset's group were a factory owner and a woman whose business dealings included cooperation with the local black market. Between them they had valuable assets, and they were able to arrange ways to contact each other safely. This would be vital to the success of the mission.

The Resistance was carried out by French people of all ages. It could be mostly passive, workers simply slowed down the pace of manufacturing goods so the invading Germans had to wait for things they needed. Some more obvious acts were printing and putting up posters urging all Frenchmen to join the Resistance. More direct sabotage, such as destroying railway lines, caused immediate disruption to the Nazi's progress. Anyone caught helping the Resistance risked torture and execution by the Germans or the Vichy French. Furthermore, the Nazis encouraged and rewarded people who turned in anyone they suspected of taking part in Resistance work. As time went on Jews were under more and more pressure. Newspapers and radio programs featured anti-Semitic propaganda and Jews were barred from many jobs. The noose was tightening.

As more local people joined Virginia's group, they worked to locate downed airmen, to see that those who were injured got medical help, and then to arm the men with accurate and up-to-date identity cards and ration cards, which they needed to travel and to buy food. Finally, her group found ways to get the men back to England. In midwinter 1942, Virginia herself accompanied one SOE agent who escaped from a hospital where he had been held as a patient. Virginia traveled with him by train to Marseille and then, the next day, to Toulon. There she found a guide who agreed to take the man across the Pyrenees. Every stage was dangerous and even making a mistake in ordering drinks at a restaurant was enough to cause an arrest.

In addition to taking care of downed airmen, Virginia's group was responsible for arranging and receiving parachute drops of agents, communication devices, medical supplies, and other things. These usually were planned to happen at night. Locations changed constantly, and planes sometimes dropped their cargo, both human and mechanical, miles from the agreed spot. At times those people and things were found by the Nazis or by German sympathizers. Once captured, prisoners were subject to harsh interrogation by the Nazis, who tried desperately to find out information about the Resistance. Because of what she knew, Virginia would be a prize catch for the Germans.

Another important responsibility of the group was gathering information about German troop movements and getting that information to London. But the Nazis were able to find radio operators quickly, using direction finders, as well as collaborators' reports. The lack of regular communication made Virginia very uneasy. A secret police force, called the Gestapo, was active throughout France. It was known as being savage and unrelenting as it hunted members of the Resistance. Once the United States entered the war in December of 1941, Virginia lost the protection she had enjoyed as a United States citizen in France. Now she was entirely at risk.

Lyons was a hub for the Resistance and a relatively safe place for Virginia to be, but at times she was required to travel. Once, accompanying an SOE man from London, she took the train to Marseille, a very difficult place for the Resistance to operate. The two were sitting in a cafe when the police raided it. One of the inspectors, who was sympathetic to the Resistance, recognized the man from SOE. He ordered his men to put the pair in a back room of the café where he knew there was a window, and he said he would interrogate them personally. As soon as they were left alone in the locked room the pair escaped through that window.

The Gestapo became aware of a woman in Lyon whose activities looked more and more suspicious. At the same time, Klaus Barbie, who worked for German Intelligence, heard of her. He was ambitious and he knew capturing that woman would give his career a great boost. Posters showing a drawing of Virginia were put up all over the area. "Find the Lady Who Limps!" Virginia was in danger.

Usually agents of SOE stayed in the field for about half a year; Virginia had been operating for thirteen months. She was reluctant to return to London, even with Dr. Rousset urging her to do so, because she knew there was much more to be done in France. Finally, in November 1942, she agreed to go. She left Lyon late one night and took the train toward Spain. There she arranged for a guide for herself and three men who also wanted to go to London. The group began its difficult journey on foot over the Pyrenees Mountains. In places the snow was deep and hard for her to manage because of her artificial leg and the heavy weight of her pack. It was not easy to breathe as they climbed higher. After two days they arrived at their destination and went to the safe houses that were waiting for them. Early the next morning they met at the town's railroad station, which was said to be safe. But police did patrol the station that day. When the four travelers could not show them proper identification, the police put them in jail. Separated from the others, when Virginia asked to see the American consul in Barcelona, her jailers just laughed at her. Her savior would be her cellmate. Virginia nursed the woman through an illness, and in return, when the woman's sentence was up she mailed a letter Virginia had written to the consulate. With the help of the consul, Virginia was finally released from prison. She was in London in time to have Christmas dinner with friends.

Gestapo members were still trying desperately to find "The lady who limps" and they arrested many of her group in Lyon, making it too dangerous for Virginia to return to France. In the spring she was sent to Spain where she found the work frustratingly slow. Disappointed, she begged to return to France but was denied. Finally, she and the SOE reached a compromise: first, she would go back to London to work as support for the agents in the field, and then she might be allowed to return to France later. She agreed, and SOE promised her special training in wireless operations. Quick and accurate communication would be critically important if the Resistance were to be successful.

In 1943 the SOE and a new American agency, The Office of Strategic Services (OSS) began working together. Virginia saw her opportunity. The staff of the OSS were new and inexperienced while she had more than a year of firsthand knowledge as an agent in France. In March 1944 the SOE reluctantly let her go and she joined the American OSS. She would go to France again.

That month Virginia and a man named Aramis crossed the English Channel by boat and then transferred to a dinghy to reach the French shore. They were to gather information about the Germans' activities, which Virginia would send back to headquarters. Things in France had become worse. The Nazis executed hundreds in retaliation for acts of sabotage by the Resistance and a new secret police group connected to the Vichy government set neighbor against neighbor. Virginia disguised herself so that she did not look anything like the sketch on posters looking for "the lady who limps." She dyed her hair gray, wore extra clothing to make herself look fat, and even had the fillings in her teeth changed to look as though they had been done by a French dentist. Most important, she spent months teaching herself to walk with slow and clumsy steps. She would not be mistaken for the limping lady again.

Virginia carried a shabby-looking suitcase, which held her wireless radio. She and Aramis made their way to Paris and then, by train and on foot, to Maidou, a small village. There she would cook and clean for a local farmer and tend his cows. In return, she would live in another house he owned and would have her meals with his family. She spoke plainly to Aramis before he left to return to Paris because she felt he talked too much, spoke too freely about himself, and he was careless in his habits. She told him firmly never to mention her but she was not sure he would pay attention. She then settled into village life. When she walked the cows to pasture each day she took care to look for fields that might be good places for parachute drops. The family grew its own food, and her small house had a loft where she could hide her radio and transmit messages. The farmer's mother made cheese for the family, and Virginia suggested she make extra portions to sell to the local German troops. Virginia could help, for she remembered making cheese at Box Horn. When she took the cheese to town to sell it, she had a chance to overhear the Germans' conversations and hoped she might learn something new about their military plans.

That suddenly changed one day when a group of Germans drove up to her doorstep. They questioned her and searched the house. She was relieved when they did not find the radio, but it had been too close a call. Within a few days Germans murdered several residents of the village and then a fellow OSS agent disappeared. It was too dangerous to stay any longer, and she radioed to London, "Wolves are at the door."

She left immediately for Paris and then went to the city of Cosne where she organized airdrops and arranged to arm and equip local groups. She moved often so that her transmission sites would be harder to locate. In late May she received a message from OSS headquarters asking for information about major movements of troops. She wanted to ask what was going on, but knew her job was to report, not to question. She did not have long to wait. The Allied forces began landing on the French coast a few days later on June 6, 1944, D-Day. She and her groups had drawn up sabotage plans and now they were told to put them into action. Knowing the Germans would want to rush men and equipment to the beach area, Virginia's groups went to work setting explosives on vital rail lines that night. Like Resistance fighters all over France, they were successful and many rail lines were destroyed, disrupting the German plans.

Next she went to meet with a group of men in the town of Chambon to see how the OSS could support them. Residents had begun helping Jews soon after Vichy France signed its treaty with Germany in 1940. Virginia built a Resistance circuit that arranged for parachute drops and organized people to meet them. Weapons, clothing, food, and medicines arrived carefully packed in cylinders along with suggestions for more acts of sabotage. Virginia continued to send and receive reports from OSS headquarters, helped her people plan to sabotage roads the Germans needed, and taught them the guerilla tactics she learned in her SOE training.

By mid-August the war in France was going much better for the Allies. Paris would soon be free of its occupiers, and suddenly everyone wanted to be counted as a member of the Resistance. Virginia's group had done well.

One of the last drops she arranged delivered two men, American lieutenants Henry Riley and Paul Goillot who brought messages and money. Virginia and her team told them the war was over in their area—there were no more Germans in the district. But the war itself was not yet over, the men argued, and they volunteered to go wherever she was going. They looked for a unit that could use their help, but finally they decided to go to Paris. They could all check in with the American headquarters there, and Paul Goillot could visit his family, who had lived in Paris throughout the war. In late September 1944, Virginia returned to London.

Attacks and counterattacks continued. The OSS wanted to work with members of the underground in Austria, and they wanted Virginia to organize and lead their effort. She and Paul Goillot, who would later become her husband, agreed to help and flew to Italy to prepare for their mission. The night before they were scheduled to go into Austria, headquarters sent a message: their mission was cancelled. On May 7, Germany surrendered. The war in Europe was over.

Virginia and Paul went to Paris then traveled to Lyon, hoping to learn what had happened to the members of the Resistance. Many of them were there, including Dr. Rousset. He told Virginia that after the Gestapo had interrogated each one of them, looking for "the limping lady," it sent them to German prison camps. When the camps were liberated and the Resistance members came home, they had nothing left, even their pots and pans had disappeared. Virginia wrote detailed reports to both the OSS and the SOE telling of the support the group had given her and asking that they be given help as they tried to start their lives all over again.

Virginia resigned from the OSS and returned to Box Horn Farm for a rest and a chance to spend time with her mother. She applied again to the State Department, still hoping to join the Foreign Service, but they answered that they were not hiring new people. She was successful in joining the newly created Central Intelligence Group (CIG) and traveled through much of Europe in 1947. The CIG was succeeded by the Central Intelligence Agency (CIA), and Virginia went to work for that agency. She and Paul Goillot married in 1950 and settled in Maryland.

Virginia ended her career with the CIA in 1966, when she turned sixty, the mandatory retirement age. She was an avid reader who belonged to several book clubs, enjoyed her family and her long-term friendships, and spent time with her dogs and working in her extensive gardens. Niece Lorna Catling remembered Virginia as "…a wonderful aunt, exotic rather than warm and cozy, and a strong person with a strong personality."[1] She spent time with her young relatives and took Lorna and her brother fishing off Solomon's Island. An adventurous cook, Virginia introduced the children to octopus and squid. While Virginia could be intimidating, her husband, Paul, was "a lot of fun, a sort of tease,"[2] recalled Ms. Catling. Their marriage seemed comfortable. She was in poor health during her last years and died in July 1982. A modest gravestone, engraved "Virginia H. Goillot, 1906-1982" marked her grave.

Her brilliant work was recognized by Britain, which awarded her the Member of the British Empire; France, which gave her the Croix de Guerre; and the United States, which awarded her the Distinguished Service Cross (DSC). She was the only civilian woman to receive the DSC during the war, and her colleagues respected her wisdom and her determination. Characteristically, Virginia refused to celebrate these honors, saying she simply did her job.

Lillie Mae Carroll Jackson, 1889-1975

Civil Rights Leader

She called herself a Freedom Fighter and some considered her the mother of the Civil Rights movement. Lillie Carroll Jackson established herself as a leading figure in the fight for racial equality in the early part of the twentieth century, long before Rosa Parks and Martin Luther King. Small in stature, Lillie became the leader of Baltimore's National Association for the Advancement of Colored People in the 1930s, when segregation was the normal way of life. How did she earn the respect of both blacks and whites in her fight against discrimination and how did she find the courage to lead the Civil Rights movement in Maryland?

Lillie's mother, Amanda Bowen, was a descendant of an African chief and an English woman whom he met on a visit to England. He married his English bride knowing that none of their children would be slaves because their mother was white. The couple came to America, settled in Montgomery County, and bought property. Their descendants became tradesmen, farmers, and like their daughter Amanda, teachers. Amanda taught school in Howard County where she met her future husband, Charles Henry Carroll. He told Amanda that he was a grandson of Charles Carroll, a signer of the Declaration of Independence, and he grew up in the family's home, Doughoreghan Manor.

Charles Henry and Amanda married in 1852 and moved to Baltimore City, where they raised their family. Lillie, the seventh of their eight children, was born in West Baltimore on Green Willow Avenue in 1889. Charles sold coal and Amanda became active in real estate. As family finances improved, they made two more moves before they settled in a large house on Druid Hill Avenue in 1903. This street was known as the place to live for middle class African Americans at that time. Amanda took in boarders and ran an ice cream parlor in the basement of the house. Known as "Miss Carroll's," it was a popular place for neighbors to stop in and share the latest news.

Lillie's parents believed in family, financial independence, education, and the church. She and her siblings attended public schools and went to Sunday services at the Sharp Street Methodist Church. As the children grew older, they had jobs. Her brother, Charles, sold newspapers for the *Afro American* and the *Baltimore Sun* and Lillie and a sister made his weekly collections for him. Lillie trained to become a teacher by spending an extra year at the Colored High and Training School. After graduating in 1908, she taught second grade at the old Biddle Street School.

Lillie met Keiffer Jackson when he was traveling through Baltimore showing religious films. By chance he stayed at the Carrolls' boardinghouse and became entranced by the young schoolteacher. She too, was attracted to the handsome man from Mississippi. Part white, part black, and part Choctaw Indian, Keiffer could have passed for a white person if he had chosen to do so. He did not. On his third visit, he proposed to Lillie and they were married at the Sharp Street Methodist Church in 1910.

For the next eight years, they traveled around the South. Keiffer showed films and Lillie, who had an excellent voice, sang ballads while he changed reels on the movie projector. To earn more money, Lillie sold programs with the words of the ballads for five cents each. Daughters Virginia, Juanita, and Marion were born during the traveling years and as they became older they joined Lillie, singing and performing skits. When Juanita was three years old, audiences were amazed by the mental telepathy act between mother and daughter. Blindfolded, Juanita sat on the stage, and described a person by using a pre-arranged numerical code. If Lillie said that she was in row five, her daughter knew that the number five meant that there was a bald man sitting in the row. Audiences called Juanita, "The Three Year Wonder."

As time went on, Lillie and Keiffer realized that traveling was not a good life for the children. They did not want them exposed to the South's racism and problems often arose because of the difference in their skin color. People thought Keiffer was white and that he should not stay in the same places as Lillie and the children. Too, they were determined that the children receive a first class education and so the family returned to Baltimore in 1919 and moved in with Amanda and Charles. Soon they welcomed a new son, Bowen, into the family.

Lillie followed Amanda's side of the family in successfully buying and owning property. She, too, bought houses in West Baltimore, which she converted into apartments and rented. She and Keiffer eventually bought a house at 1320 Eutaw Place and when Keiffer stopped showing films, he helped Lillie with her business. Owning your own house was important, Lillie told her children. Paying taxes made one independent.

The returning couple found that the racial barriers in Baltimore were not as rigid as the Deep South's because Maryland was a buffer state between north and south and many of its citizens shared the north's more lenient feelings about segregation. After the Civil War, newly freed southern blacks came to the port city to find jobs and for many years the city had a large free black population. Everyone lived by the code, separate but equal.

But equality did not exist. The Jackson children used textbooks, often with missing pages, that had been discarded by schools attended by white children. Institutions of higher learning in Maryland did not accept black students. Black teachers were not paid as much as white teachers and blacks could not apply for many of the city's municipal jobs. Blacks could not enter stores owned by white people.

Lillie began to speak out. She knew that her protests would receive more recognition if she had the support of the black clergy. Although she was a member of the Sharp Street United Methodist Church, she regularly attended five or six different church services every Sunday because she did not want to appear as if she favored one minister. Lillie had gained confidence from the years she spent traveling with Keiffer, and she was not afraid to speak in church, often interrupting the ministers.

People respected Lillie and knew that they could count on her for help. If family members were in trouble with the law, they knew that they could call "Ma Jackson" at any hour and that she would go with them to talk with police officials. Likewise, she never hesitated to wake others if she needed their help. She was developing a reputation as an articulate speaker and a woman who knew how to organize people and get things done.

Segregation issues became personal when it came time for Lillie's daughters to attend college in 1927. She was incensed that the University of Maryland would not accept Juanita, who had graduated with honors from Douglass High School, because of her skin color. Virginia's application was turned down at the Maryland Institute of Art for the same reason. Morgan State College was in its early phase of development and was without a building in which to teach. Sharp Street Church welcomed the new institution and Juanita took her first college classes in the basement of the church. But the college was not accredited and Lillie soon withdrew her daughter.

Like other black families in Baltimore considering colleges at the time, Lillie took the girls to Philadelphia where there was no racial discrimination in institutions of higher learning. Lillie was angry when Temple University would not give Juanita credit for the courses she had taken at Morgan and she promptly went to the Dean at the University of Pennsylvania where the courses were accepted and her bright daughter was admitted. Virginia went to the Philadelphia Museum and School of Art. While Virginia found her courses hard, Juanita flourished in her academic environment. The sisters loved the freedom they experienced in their new surroundings. They could enter many places such as restaurants, museums, and movie theaters that were off limits to them at home.

When the girls returned to Baltimore in 1931 they saw no improvement in the city's racial climate. With Lillie's backing and the encouragement of Carl Murphy, the owner of the *Afro American Newspaper,* the girls organized a group called the Forum. Again, Lillie reached out to the black clergy for support and arranged for the Forum to meet at the Sharp Street Church every Friday. It was similar to an open university. Young blacks from all economic levels went to the Forum to hear people speak about many issues such as lynchings and jobs. When a black man was lynched on the Eastern Shore of Maryland, people were outraged. Lillie urged Forum members to gather signatures to support an anti-lynching bill. She made countless phone calls and wrote many letters to state senators in protest.

Lillie also organized the group to boycott the local A&P grocery store, which did not hire black people but certainly wanted their business. The "Buy Where You Can Work" protest was successful. When white storeowners began losing business, they gave in. It was a huge victory—Lillie and her followers were beginning to break down the wall of discrimination.

In 1935 Carl Murphy asked Lillie to head Baltimore's chapter of the National Association for the Advancement of Colored People (NAACP), which had grown weak over the years. She had never been a member of the NAACP but she realized that the organization, along with the support of the *Afro American* and the clergy, was the best way to fight the battles that lay ahead. She persuaded many people to join the NAACP, and under her leadership, the Baltimore branch became the largest in the country and one of the most prominent. The majority of the members were black but many white people joined as well. Lillie did not hesitate to charge each member one dollar to join and she did not hesitate to change the rules for the NAACP's board membership. Because she liked working with ordinary people, Lillie made sure that board members came from all walks of life. Previously, only professionals such as doctors or lawyers were eligible. Everyone had the same interests and goals she said. Judge Robert Watts of Baltimore told a friend, "Lillie united people around things that no one could oppose."[1]

A malformation on her face did not stop Lillie from making public appearances. When she was a young woman she developed an infection in the mastoid bone, which is located behind the ear. Misdiagnosed by a doctor, she then went to see Dr. Crow at Johns Hopkins. He removed a great deal of bone mass and later told her, "I took more bone, decayed bone, and infection than from any human head I've seen at Hopkins."[2] Perhaps there was nerve damage as well, but the operation left Lillie with a disfigured left cheek. She could no longer smile, and when she was photographed she made sure to turn the bad cheek away from the camera.

Before the operation Lillie made a promise to God that if she survived she would dedicate her life to his work. Lillie kept that promise. Firmly believing that Freedom Fighters were members of God's army, Lillie and her followers began the battle to eliminate injustices for all people. A strong believer in the United States Constitution and in non-violence, she urged NAACP members to fight within the law. Be persistent and speak out loud and clear, she told them. If anyone's constitutional rights were threatened, Lillie and the NAACP were there to defend them.

The NAACP's Legal Defense Fund enabled Lillie to hire the best lawyers and courtrooms became the arenas for settling disputes. In 1935, when Charles Houston and his assistant, Thurgood Marshall, defeated the Law School of the University of Maryland's policy of not allowing black students to enroll, NAACP members were ecstatic. These two lawyers from Howard University in Washington, DC, claimed that the 14th Amendment to the United States Constitution made the University's policy illegal. It was a momentous victory and encouraged the black community to continue its fight for equality.

Hiring practices, pay scales, and access to public places improved somewhat in the 1940s. It was no longer legal to pay black teachers less than white teachers. Golf courses were open to all races. Later, public parks and swimming pools would open their doors to everyone. Blacks could take the civil service exam and if they did well, they were eligible for jobs in the police force. Lillie started classes to prepare applicants for the exam. The Enoch Pratt Library opened its training program to all citizens.

Lillie acted on her beliefs. After learning that the bank she used would not change its policy in loaning money to blacks to start their businesses, she promptly closed her account and went to another bank. Later when Dr. Winifred Bryson, an economics professor at Morgan, who also kept the financial records for the NAACP, opened the Advance Savings and Loan Association, Lillie urged NAACP members to open accounts there. Very soon the new institution received more than enough deposits to be accredited. When Lillie felt that something was "ungodly," she badgered her opponent relentlessly until things were settled in her favor. An unrelenting warrior in the fight to abolish lynching, she spoke to numerous groups and wrote numerous letters.

In the 1940s and 1950s the NAACP focused on voter registration. Blacks were required to sign a declaration of intention to vote, but it was not easy for them. Designated locations were difficult to get to, and were often in the courthouse, a place that most black people chose to avoid. Too, operation hours were 9 A.M. to 4 P.M., not convenient times for a working person. Lillie and Carl Murphy persuaded local businesses to provide funds so that they could hire students to go door-to-door getting people to sign the petition for voting privileges. Lillie told people that the only way to fight segregation was to vote because votes change laws. She instigated marches to spread the word. It was not until President Lyndon Johnson signed the voter registration bill of 1965 that African Americans could vote without any interference. It was every citizen's constitutional right to choose his or her leaders in America, he said.

In the 1950s Lillie gained the help and admiration of Theodore McKeldin. A white man, he was twice mayor of Baltimore and once governor of Maryland. Both he and Lillie believed in the brotherhood of man and they worked well together. Lillie brought issues to his attention and he had the political power to make changes. He was the first mayor to appoint blacks to prominent positions in city government. As governor, he integrated the cafeteria in the Governor's mansion because he simply would not allow separate dining areas for black and white employees and no one argued with him. Lillie organized picket lines in front of the Ford Theater to protest its policy of not allowing blacks in the audience. This public demonstration continued for seven years, but it was not until Governor McKeldin joined the protest that the theater opened its doors to African Americans. Lillie often called him, so much so that when he was Governor, he told an aide to give Lillie whatever she wanted. He'd rather have the devil after him than Mrs. Jackson.

Just like the doors to her mother's ice cream parlor, Lillie's doors were always open to callers. One son-in-law remembered that as family members left for work every morning, visitors took their places at the breakfast table and talked about a range of subjects, not necessarily those concerning the NAACP. If the phone rang, Lillie answered and would engage in long conversations. Guests learned to expect that.

Ma Jackson had strong feelings about drinking alcohol and smoking, she did not allow either in her house. Once when Walter White, a board member of the National NAACP, came for dinner and he started to light a cigarette, Lillie immediately said, "Oh Mr. White, you can't smoke in my home. This is a Christian home."[3] She also formed the Northwest Baltimore Protective Association to keep taverns and barbershops from opening in residential neighborhoods. Another Baltimore civil rights activist and State Senator, Verda Welcome, joined her in this endeavor and recalled that Lillie wanted to instill pride in the black community.

Income from Lillie's properties allowed the Jacksons' life to be comfortable but not opulent. There was money for education and travel but fancy clothes and jewelry were not for this matriarch. She only wore them if they were gifts from family members. While Lillie frowned on dancing, she would attend a play if asked and she enjoyed reading and traveling. She never missed a national meeting of the NAACP, and periodically traveled to Europe, always by ship. While abroad, she chose to stay with friends rather than in hotels. She enjoyed cultural outings and seeing new places, but she was always glad to return home. One daughter remembered that on a return trip from abroad, Lillie sang *America the Beautiful* as the ship sailed by the Statue of Liberty.

Some may have thought Lillie Carroll Jackson was too aggressive and ahead of her time, but she was an unstoppable force in moving the Civil Rights movement forward. She passed the legacy to her family and today family members continue the fight and emphasize the importance of freedom and equality for all people. Through energy, hard work, and a positive approach to problems, she was able to build on the strength of the black community and break barriers.

Claire McCardell, 1905-1958
Fashion Designer

Claire McCardell wearing Claire McCardell

As a young girl, Claire McCardell made paper dolls from photographs in her mother's fashion magazines. She loved to rearrange their outfits, improving them, she said. With an eye for fashion and a sense of practicality, Claire would become the creator of the "American Look." This look moved American women beyond structured, corseted styles into clothes that were comfortable and functional, as well as stylish. What led this young woman from Frederick, Maryland, to have the courage to make her way in New York City and become a legendary clothes designer? The Claire McCardell story was one of determination, talent, and success.

Everyone in the small Maryland town knew and respected the McCardells. Adrian Leroy McCardell was a state senator, president of the Frederick State Bank, and an elder in the Evangelical and Reformed Church. When people saw him walking around town, they saw an impeccably dressed man in well-tailored suits. He met his wife, Eleanore Clingan, who was from Jackson, Mississippi, when she was visiting her cousins. They married, settled in Frederick, and raised four children, Claire, Adrian, Robert, and John. Eleanore was well-read, gracious, and fashionable. Claire would use many aspects of her parents' styles in her designs.

Claire's mother enjoyed wearing the latest styles and subscribed to various fashion magazines from which she chose the dresses she liked. Annie Koogle, the family seamstress, came to the house twice a year to make Eleanore's dresses and to do general sewing for the family. During these visits Claire spent hours watching the seamstress choose and drape fabrics before she went to the sewing machine. It was under her guidance that Claire gained firsthand knowledge of garment construction, how the individual pattern pieces are put together.

In high school Claire often designed her own clothes from sketches she made of costumes that she saw at Washington's National Theater. Some promptly received a negative vote from the family. The McCardells regularly attended church and people looked forward to seeing what Claire wore as she had a habit of adding the unusual to her outfits. A brother recalled that one Sunday morning she came down the steps wearing a hat that everyone in the family thought was too "flashy." When they refused to go to church with her, she took it off and wore something more appropriate.

Claire was not a strong student but she excelled in sports. Her friends called her "Kick," for her tomboyish nature and her ability to defend herself from her three younger brothers. Whether playing in the neighborhood or participating in sports, she often borrowed her brothers' clothes, and she commented on how much more practical they were to wear than skirts. She especially liked the deep pockets in their trousers—a feature that she later incorporated into her designs. One brother remembered that it was not uncommon for him and his brothers to look for a pair of pants or shirt only to find that their sister was dissecting the garments to learn more about their construction. Durable fabrics and clothing that allowed women to move freely became part of the McCardell style.

When Claire graduated from high school, she told her parents that she wanted to study fashion and go to New York. Her father vetoed this request because he thought his sixteen-year-old daughter was far too young to leave home. So Claire attended Hood College in Frederick, a school whose founders included her paternal grandfather. She did not do well in her studies and after the second year she withdrew from the college. She was determined to go to New York City and study design.

With her mother's help, Claire convinced her father to allow her to go to New York and she enrolled in what is now Parsons The New School for Design. She roomed with two other girls at the Three Arts Club, an organization supported by wealthy patrons who hosted cultural events and provided housing for those interested in the arts. Claire and her friends were thrilled to learn that the patrons held rummage sales where they sold their gently used clothing, most of which were made by designers in Paris. Claire bought as many dresses as she could and just as when she was a child, she took them apart and studied each item's structural technique before hand sewing them back together.

Although Claire loved New York and Parsons, she did not do well in her first year courses. Knowing that students in their second year could study costume design at the school's extension in Paris, she convinced the teacher that if she went abroad her grades would improve. The instructor agreed. Later he commented that she was a very determined young lady.

Once again, her mother helped Claire negotiate her father's concerns about her travels and Claire went to Paris in 1926 to study design. She wrote almost daily to her parents. In a letter dated August 27, 1926, Claire wrote, "…got here this afternoon about five o'clock and just love it but don't think much of the looks of French men."[1] And later, "Went to school this morning and just love it."[2] Proud of her French, she wrote, "I can make them understand real well and a Frenchman even told me I was good at it. I thought I hadn't learned much last year but I learned loads."[3] Her first assignment, she wrote, was to design a booklet cover for the Luxembourg Gardens in comic book style.

She got a part time job as an intern for a company that hired students to copy and trace designs from top couturiers. From these sketches the company reproduced Paris dresses at reasonable prices. The internship provided another opportunity for Claire to learn more about clothing construction.

Claire remained an average student, but she blossomed as she discovered Paris. She and her classmates scouted the city's flea markets for discarded French clothing and bought year-end samples from major designers. Disassembling and resembling each frock became a favorite pastime for the girls. It was during this time that Claire became acquainted with the designs of Madeline Vionnet, one of the leading dressmakers of the twentieth century. Madeline Vionnet had a unique way of handling fabrics. She cut them diagonally rather than up and down or straight across. Called the bias cut, Claire would use this technique often.

Claire graduated from Parsons in 1928 and set out to enter the design world in New York. Except for a few insignificant jobs such as painting roses on lampshades, rejections were endless for the first five years. When Claire developed pneumonia her mother urged her to come home and recuperate. She did, but her father's suggestion that she become a teacher led Claire back to New York in less than a week. She would find a job in design.

The city's leading department store, B. Altman, hired her as a model. At 5 feet 7 inches in height, Claire was a natural for wearing clothes and a natural to represent the American girl. She walked with a slouchy hip-forward style that she later taught to her own models. Her time at B. Altman's exposed her to the inner world of New York fashion and gave her a chance to see the latest techniques used by European designers. Years later, she joked that she was spying, not modeling.

In 1930 the designer Robert Turk hired her as his assistant. When his business floundered it was taken over by the sportswear company, Townley Frocks. When Robert Turk died in a swimming accident in 1931 the company asked Claire to finish the fall line. People liked the "McCardellisms," Claire's distinct styling features that included pockets, top-stitching, various symmetrical closures, wrap ties, spaghetti straps, and bias cut skirts made of unusual fabrics such as stripes, plaids, and denim. Townley was pleased with the sales and as a result the company made Claire a lead designer. As such she traveled to Paris twice a year to see the latest fashions. She knew that she was supposed to copy what she saw, and she did, but she thought the French clothes were too constricted for comfortable wear. While abroad she visited other European cities and took note of trends, one of which was the Austrian dirndl. Claire liked the full, free-flowing skirt and it was a popular item in her collection for the next two years. She never beaded or embroidered her clothes, but her models often wore strands of beads or colored glass which she had collected on these trips.

Toward the end of her time at Townley, she designed the "Monastic dress." This flowing tent-like, bias cut dress with attached ties could be wrapped as each woman liked. It could be long or day length and it was a staple in Claire's collections. However, the Monastic dress sold so quickly that Townley did not have time to patent the design. The company spent many hours at a great expense to fight knock-offs. Claire wrote her parents:

"My dress is still causing more excitement. Every one we've made sold…and in the meantime all the manufacturers of 7th Avenue seem to have copied it and we spend our time proving that it's my original."[4] Financial difficulties resulted and Townley Frocks closed. Claire was once more looking for work.

Hattie Carnegie, a well-known designer, hired her, and Claire wrote her parents, "I'm going to work for Hattie Carnegie. Now that I've made up my mind I'm very excited about it. It just seems to be too good to be true. I can make all the crazy clothes I've never been able to make at Townley's."[5] Although Claire took what was useful in Paris designs and made them into clothes that American women could wear, Hattie Carnegie's patrons wanted Parisian couture. Claire's clothes were too simple.

By 1940 Townley Frocks planned to reopen. On a chance meeting, Claire shared an elevator with the past head of Townley and Adrian Klein, the new head of the company. Claire wished them well, but before she left the elevator, Adrian Klein asked Claire to return to Townley Frocks. Claire agreed, but only under certain conditions. There were to be absolutely no changes made to her designs and they would all carry the C McC.

label. This was a first. No other American designer had his or her own private label. She also requested that changes be made to the showroom. The walls were to be painted in different colors, one black, one navy, and one beige. A shiny linoleum floor would replace the existing wooden one. These surroundings, she thought, would provide an excellent backdrop when she showed her collections to clients and the press.

Designers envied Claire McCardell's freedom at Townley. She created what she wanted and did not have to justify the expense for extra material if she needed it. She never attended another Paris fashion show because she did not want to be influenced by them. As a way of breaking away from the structured look of Parisian designs, she eliminated shoulder pads in her dresses. Townley did not censure this new look, but promptly assured its patrons that shoulder pads could be inserted if the wearer desired. At this time most designers specialized and made just one type of garment, which required buyers to visit many showrooms in New York City's garment center. Claire designed a wide variety of items from raincoats and bathing suits to evening gowns. Smaller retailers liked the convenience of finding everything in one location and Townley prospered.

For Claire, clothes had to have a reason and many of her ideas came about because of her own needs. In order to cut down on the number of suitcases she needed when she traveled abroad, she came up with a line of interchangeable separates. Although Claire wore them often, it took American women several years to appreciate the separates system. Her ears got cold when she skied and she created the Superman hood in 1942. This jersey headpiece could be rolled up over the head or down as the wearer wished. Once aboard an ocean liner, she became cold in her evening dress. This led her to create an evening wrap made out of tweed, a material usually used for men's clothing. Unlike most designers, Claire often reused shapes and pieces from her collections—just in different forms. Her dresses never appeared out of date and they could be worn for years with just a change in hemline lengths.

In 1941 America entered World War II. As men left to fight, women joined the workforce and their clothing needs changed. Claire realized that fancy frocks from Paris were not practical, nor were they available. French designers had closed their doors. When the US government issued restrictions to the garment industry, Claire became inventive and made her mark in the fashion world. She made reasonably priced, stylish clothing from sturdy yet easy to care for fabrics, such as denim, heavy cotton, and jersey. She visited mills in the South and looked for alternative fabrics such as mattress ticking, children's prints, and even butcher apron material. At one point there was a surplus of weather balloon cotton and Claire bought all she could. Her wrap and tie dresses eliminated the need for metal zippers and enabled each individual to create a waistline most flattering to her. When shoe leather was rationed, Claire responded by working with Capezio, a man whose company made ballet slippers for dancers. She supplied him with material samples that matched her collection and when her models appeared wearing color-coordinated flats they were an immediate hit. Capezio began to make flat shoes. American women adapted to the changes and felt patriotic when they wore Claire's clothes.

During these years Claire designed two practical dresses for the American woman, who no longer had domestic help. One was the kitchen dinner dress. It was a full-skirted shirtwaist dress with its own matching apron. This combination allowed women to remove the apron when they left the kitchen and appear presentable when their guests arrived. When Harper's Bazaar asked her to design a fashionable dress for women to wear when doing housework, Claire created the Popover dress. It was a simple wrap-front denim dress that included its own apron as well as an attached oven mitt. In 1941 women placed 75,000 orders for the $6.95 dress. Modified each season, it remained part of Claire's permanent collection. In order to avoid the problems of the Monastic dress, Townley's copyrighted the Popover for three years.

The war and mass production of clothing were boosts to Claire's career. In 1942 she received the American Fashion Critics' Award, which acknowledged the success of her designs despite the war restrictions. Townley's sales skyrocketed and in just ten years, people recognized Claire as a major designer.

In 1944 she married a long time suitor, Irving Drought Harris, whom she had met on an ocean liner while on one of her Parisian buying trips. Harris was divorced with two young boys; Claire took her time before she introduced him to her parents because she feared their disapproval. The couple became part of New York's social whirl, but their favorite times were spent at an old farmhouse in Frenchtown, New Jersey.

After the war, the fashion industry thought American women would return to the Paris fashion houses, but this did not happen. The war years allowed these women to become independent and they knew what they wanted to wear. Claire's clothes provided women with outfits they could wear driving carpools, as well as going to lunch, and her sportswear was fun and comfortable. When she designed the "diaper bathing suit" it caused quite a stir. This was one piece of material that one wrapped around the body looking very much like its namesake. People thought her bathing suits were too daring because they did not have padding and were skintight. Claire sharply responded that a bathing suit was just what the name implied. She was the first to use elasticized material from which she created tube tops. She was not afraid to make a playsuit out of silk just as she was not afraid to make an evening wrap out of tweed.

During the early 1950s, Claire lent her name to other products such as sunglasses and gloves. She began a jewelry line, produced dress patterns for the home seamstress and Claire McCardell paper dolls for the younger set. Companies wanted her to endorse their products—everything from playing cards to white bread. She agreed to design practical yet attractive clothing for the Fuller Brush Company with the hope of changing women's minds about what they wore when cleaning house—their outfits could be as sleek as the cleaning utensils.

Claire received many accolades during her career. Despite her growing reputation, she was a shy woman and the awards always surprised her. In 1943 The Mademoiselle Merit Award was given to her for designing many firsts, her "McCardellisms." In 1944 she received the Coty American Fashion Critics Award and the Best Designer Sportswear Award, followed by the Neiman Marcus Award in 1948. In 1950 President Harry S. Truman handed her an award given by the Women's Press Club. She was quite proud of the fact that she was the first fashion designer to be honored by the organization.

Vogue and *Harpers Bazaar*, two prominent fashion magazines, followed her career with many stories and photographs. In 1955 *Life* magazine asked Claire to fly to Europe to create a wardrobe made from fabrics that had been designed by leading artists such as Chagall, Picasso, Miro, and Dufy. She found it hard to believe that she was designing outfits that would be sold at reasonable prices on fabrics designed by artists whose works sold for thousands of dollars. This was a first for any designer and it increased interest in Claire McCardell clothing.

The same year *Time* magazine put her on its cover, making her one of only three fashion designers to have that honor. Recognizing Claire's influence on sportswear, *Time* also asked her to help create a new magazine, *Sports Illustrated*. The following year, she co-authored a book called *What Shall I Wear?* Despite her successful career she also found time to advise students. She was an active alumna at Parsons and became a member of its board. In 1954 she created the Claire McCardell Golden Thimble Award for the student with the most promising designs.

Claire McCardell died of cancer in 1958 at the age of 53. Admiration for the designer and her clothes remained. They were highly collectible and sold for far more than they did when they were first made. Many considered her clothes timeless. Today's designers have included "McCardellisms" such as bias cut skirts, spaghetti straps, and tailored trousers in their looks. People have seen many of her dresses in the Costume Collection at the Metropolitan Museum of Art and the Fashion Institute of Technology, as well as at other museums. There have been several exhibitions of her fashions since her death. In 2001 New York City created a Fashion Walk of Fame on Seventh Avenue, the fashion center of the city, to honor the leaders of the fashion world. Claire McCardell's name was installed on one of the bronze plaques.

Barbara Ann Mikulski, 1936-
US Senator

Barbara Mikulski

Barbara Mikulski lived the American Dream. She grew up in a closely-knit Polish neighborhood in Southeast Baltimore where she learned the value of an honest day's work, the value of being a good neighbor, and the value of being a member of the community. The oldest of three girls, she often helped her father in the grocery store near their home. She knew that he opened his store early in the morning so that the steelworkers in the neighborhood could buy their lunch before they started their morning shift. If customers were unable to come to the store to pick up their groceries, Barbara delivered them to their door. Down the street was her grandparent's bakery, the first Polish-owned bakery in Baltimore. Barbara has always been proud of her ethnicity and her background helped her understand issues that confronted minorities and immigrants.

In 2004 Barbara Mikulski was elected to her fourth term as United States Senator from Maryland, making her the most senior female Senator. She has achieved many firsts in her career. She was the first Democratic woman elected to the Senate on her own merits. She was the first Democratic woman elected to both houses of Congress and the first woman to win a statewide election in her home state, Maryland. How did the granddaughter of Polish immigrants achieve these firsts? And what made her so popular with her constituents who called her "Senator Barb?"

Her success never surprised her parents. Even when she was a young girl, Barbara had the ability to get others to follow her. She was not athletic and rather than skin her knees skipping rope or playing tag, she persuaded friends and cousins to perform in plays that she wrote and directed. She gathered neighbors and family to see the productions held in the Mikulski's garage.

At the Catholic schools she and her sisters attended, Barbara learned good study habits. She loved reading and that led her to recognize literacy as a key element in education. She was a member of the Girl Scouts, an organization that instilled self-confidence and encouraged young girls to reach for their goals. Girls could do anything if they tried. That message was not lost on Barbara.

As all young people do, Barbara thought about what she wanted to be when she grew up. As a result of her Catholic education, Barbara thought she might become a nun. She was impressed by their devotion to helping others, but she realized that she was too outspoken to adhere to the rules of a convent. After seeing a movie about Marie Curie, Barbara briefly thought about becoming a scientist. Marie Curie was Polish and the first woman to win the Nobel Prize for discovering radioactive substances. Certainly the scientist's Polish heritage impressed Barbara, but when she received a "C" in chemistry and an "A" in sociology, she said, "I decided to go with my strengths and to help others. That's why I became a social worker."[1] Her Catholic education also exposed her to the Christopher movement, which emphasized helping others. After receiving a Bachelor's degree in sociology from Mount St. Agnes College, now Loyola College, in 1958, she received a Master's degree in social work from the University of Maryland in 1965.

Barbara began working at the Associated Catholic Charities and then at the Baltimore Department of Social Services. She honed her organization and leadership skills when the Department of Social Services put her in charge of decentralizing welfare programs in 1966. Here she saw the horrors of child neglect and abuse. The impression was lasting and she became a strong advocate for families and children. Knowing how hard it was for senior citizens to understand the Medicare program, she spent many hours helping them negotiate the system.

Many nationalities lived in and around Barbara's neighborhood. The city's first area where African Americans could own homes was in nearby Fells Point and when Baltimore City wanted to build a sixteen-lane highway through this section of the city in 1968, Barbara was furious. She became a warrior and organized groups from various parts of the city to fight the proposed highway. Despite opposition from the City Council, Barbara and her supporters defeated the proposal. This reinforced her belief in community activism. With victory in her voice, she declared, "The British couldn't take Fells Point, the termites couldn't take Fells Point, and damn if we'll let the State Roads Commission take Fells Point!"[2] Barbara decided to change careers. "Winning the road fight was my turning point—when I knew I would rather be opening doors for others from the inside, than knocking on doors from the outside."[3]

Barbara's concern over problems that immigrants faced led her to write, "Who Speaks for Ethnic America?" for the *New York Times* in 1970. She stated that although immigrants built America, the establishment treated them badly. Because of their speech and other cultural differences, people made fun of them. Society did not award them the privileges it gave to people in banking and education. They organized labor unions in order to improve wages and working conditions and Barbara supported those unions.

In 1971 she ran for a seat on the Baltimore City Council. She had no experience and no political backing, but she was a fighter and knew how to talk to people. During the campaign she knocked on thousands of doors in and around her neighborhood and in doing so wore out five pairs of shoes. She built coalitions and firmly believed that if people worked together, they could make changes. People listened to her and she won the election.

As a member of Baltimore's City Council, she maintained the respect of the city's ethnic groups. For the five years she was on the Council, her constituents went to her with their problems. They knew that Barbara was one of them, that she would listen, and that she would act. She became more interested in politics and ran for the House of Representatives in 1974. It was the only election that she ever lost. Nevertheless, her reputation as an activist grew, as did the number of her supporters. Their backing was so strong that when Democrat Paul Sarbanes announced his candidacy for the US Senate in 1976, Barbara Mikulski was elected to serve Maryland's third district in the US House of Representatives. Her philosophy of being available to constituents, listening to them, and supporting them would be Barbara's strength throughout her career

When Barbara first arrived as a member of the House of Representatives in 1977, Congress recognized her leadership qualities and placed her on important committees, which gave her the opportunity to promote issues favorable to Marylanders. As a member of the Merchant Marine and Fisheries Committee she addressed concerns related to Baltimore's port. She was the first woman appointed to the House Energy and Commerce Committee, one of the most powerful in Congress. There she became involved with railroads, telecommunications, and health care. She pushed for important legislation and championed the Child Abuse Act and Equal Rights for Women. A self-proclaimed feminist, she developed the reputation as being "feisty" whenever she dealt with issues concerning children or women. She served as a congresswoman for ten years.

In 1986 Barbara decided to run for the Senate when Charles Mathias, Jr. retired. This was not an easy decision for her. She was comfortable in the House of Representatives, but she knew she could do more as a Senator. Would she be elected? She remembered what her great grandmother said, "There were no guarantees in life, only opportunities,"[4] and she declared her candidacy.

Despite running against a well-connected Republican opponent, Barbara won the election. She did it the same way she stopped the highway in Fells Point. She gathered all her supporters, arranged meetings with important leaders in business and politics, and campaigned—relentlessly. Barbara realized that she had to improve her image if she was going to get more votes than her opponent, Linda Chavez, who was a polished, personable, and accomplished woman. With the help of a makeup advisor who had worked with presidential candidates, Barbara learned how to wear the right lip gloss for television cameras and how to improve her television manner. She bought more stylish clothes, more flattering eyeglasses, and she lost over forty pounds.

Yes, now she was a Senator. But how could she succeed within that primarily male dominated group? There were no guidelines. Barbara did what she had done in the past. She asked for advice from important leaders in the Senate and she did her homework and went to meetings—on time. She attended hearings and went on fact-finding trips with other senators. She developed a reputation as being reliable and leaders recognized her determination and the speed with which she grasped core issues. As a result, Barbara was assigned to two important committees, the Senate Appropriations Committee, which oversaw the budget, and the Education and Labor Committee.

Senator Barb worked tirelessly for Maryland citizens. She fought for the working people and for the creation of more jobs in the state. She obtained funding for the Beltsville Agricultural Research Center and for oyster beds, an important industry for Maryland. She helped get more money for the mass transit system and for maintaining a weather station on the Eastern Shore. The Senator remembered summers spent on Stoney Creek, just off the Chesapeake Bay, when the water was much cleaner and the crabs were abundant. She fondly recalled that as a young girl she shocked her friends by catching fish, decapitating them, and using their heads for crab bait. Hoping that future generations could enjoy a healthy bay with plenty of crabs, she supported the clean up of the Chesapeake Bay.

Leaders of the Democratic Party asked Barbara to address its Presidential Convention in 1992 to introduce Hillary Clinton as the next First Lady. This greatly increased her visibility. She gave a rousing speech about the four women newly elected to the Senate and how proud she was that more women were running for public office. Reelected to the Senate that year, she continued to improve her leadership skills. Friends and foes alike regarded her as one of the most influential senators on Capitol Hill.

A consistent advocate for issues relating to Maryland, she also took on issues that affect all Americans. She fought for senior citizens, and she supported Medicaid's prescription program and the Spousal Anti-Poverty Act. This Act helped older people avoid bankruptcy when it was necessary to send a spouse to a nursing home. She knew how difficult it was to care for sick relatives. Barbara and her sisters shared responsibilities for their mother after their father died. It was not an easy time for any of them, especially Barbara, who traveled to Washington each day.

A tireless advocate for women, she fought for equal rights and especially equal pay. She lobbied insurance companies to pay for annual mammograms for all women, beginning at age forty. She co-sponsored the Homemaker IRA, which allowed stay at home mothers to put money in a tax-deferred account just like mothers working outside the home. Barbara's negotiation skills once more became apparent when she got the other women senators to back her. As a united front, regardless of their political party, they made their male counterparts aware of the importance of issues relating to women. Many times favorable legislation was the result.

Barbara supported the creation of the Department of Homeland Security, worked for more funding for the Environmental Protection Agency, and was a valued member of the Senate's Ethics Committee. She believed in the importance of space exploration and was successful in obtaining additional financial support for the National Aeronautics and Space Administration (NASA). In May 2007 Barbara was host to Great Britain's Queen Elizabeth II and her husband, Prince Philip. In her speech she discussed the value of space exploration and gave the royal couple a photograph taken by the Hubble Space Telescope.

To make sure there would be no digital divide in America she became committed to preparing students for future jobs. She worked to get more money for math and science education through the National Science Foundation. She supported updating school curricula. She created Space Hope, a combined effort between NASA and the Greater Baltimore Alliance, to renovate the American Can Company building in Baltimore to house a program that would enable young people to learn the latest technology. She supported the creation of community technology centers so that all citizens could be computer literate. She and Senator Benjamin Cardin were instrumental in getting Congress to give four million dollars to support broadband capability for the Eastern Shore of Maryland, which would allow students and businesses there to connect to the information highway.

As one of the longest serving female senators, Barbara Mikulski became known as the Dean of Senate Women. When she first arrived on Capitol Hill, she was one of two female senators. By 2009, with the beginning of the 111th Congress, there were seventeen. Although they might disagree on issues, they supported and learned from each other. She was an important member of the Congresswoman's Caucus, which she helped establish when she was a member of the House of Representatives. Proud to mentor newcomers, Barbara took on the responsibility of guiding them as they found their voices in the Senate. When a group of five new female senators was elected in 1992, Barbara greeted them with manuals that she had written. In each was an ABC list of how to get things accomplished in the Senate, how to work with both parties to get bills approved, and how to get placed on committees where they could do the most for their constituents. Nothing like that had ever been done before and the women were grateful. Barbara emphasized the importance of having guiding principles for their office staff. Knowing they were part of history, they wanted to encourage more women to run for public office. In 2001, when there were only nine female senators, they wrote a book, *Nine and Counting: The Women of the Senate,* in which they each described the challenges they faced. Proceeds from the book went to the Girl Scouts of America, the organization that Barbara credited for fostering her leadership skills.

"Senator Barb" was a grass roots politician. She had strong ties to her neighborhood and returned to Baltimore each evening. She knew her strengths and supporters. Possessing a good sense of humor and a quick understanding of issues, she earned the respect of her congressional colleagues. She made an effort to look at issues from a broad perspective and she was a role model for hard work, honesty, and caring.

Sadie Kneller Miller, 1867-1920
Photojournalist

Sadie Kneller Miller in the Rocky Mountains

Westminster, Maryland, a country town not far from Baltimore, was the childhood home of Sarah "Sadie" Kneller. Sadie's grandfather owned a lumber mill and townspeople regarded the Miller family as prominent members of the community. Sadie was an only child and grew up in a house in the center of Westminster. The surrounding land, which was primarily devoted to farming, provided a gentle setting for Sadie's childhood. Who would have guessed that this small girl from this small town would travel all over the world as the first woman photojournalist in the early part of the 20th century? Or that people would eagerly look forward to reading her adeptly written stories and exciting photographs that she sent to *Leslie's Illustrated Weekly?* Or that foreign newspapers would also pick up her articles? Sadie had a love of adventure, spunk, and the determination to do well.

Sadie Miller attended elementary and high school in Westminster before continuing on to the local college, Western Maryland, now McDaniel College. She excelled in English and public speaking. A woman with a good sense of humor, she had the ability to tell a good story, could mimic almost anyone, and local groups often asked her to speak. She thought of becoming a writer but the theater interested her as well. However, her parents disapproved of acting as a profession, so Sadie took her first job at the town's newspaper, the *Westminster Democratic Advocate.* The paper's editor gave her two pieces of advice that she never forgot: never let your ego interfere with reporting, and be as concise as possible when writing.

In 1894 Sadie married Charles R. Miller, whom she had met at college. Charles played on the college's baseball team and their courtship revolved around his baseball games. As Sadie watched, she became quite knowledgeable about the game's finer points. Shortly after they married, they moved to Baltimore where Charles had taken a job with the Fidelity and Trust Company. Charles came from a wealthy family and was able to build a house on Eutaw Place, a fashionable area of the city.

Her knowledge of baseball from her courtship days led her to a job covering the Orioles games for the *Baltimore Telegram.* Readers loved her wit and accurate reporting. Even *The Washington Post* took note, saying that other newspapers often quoted the adept reporter from Baltimore. But no one knew Sadie was a woman. At the time she was the only woman to cover sports for a newspaper and, in order to hide her gender, she signed her articles S.K.M. After one game between the Orioles and the New York Giants, she asked to interview one of the Giants players, Andy Freeman. Expecting a he rather than a she, he commented that she was a woman. Sadie smiled and responded, "I certainly hope so."[1]

Around the turn of the century, Sadie became interested in photography. When friends commented on the excellence of her pictures, she responded that if she did anything, she wanted to do it well or not at all. In 1898 she took a photograph of three Spanish sailors who were prisoners at the Naval Academy in Annapolis, Maryland, during the Spanish American War and submitted it to *Leslie's Illustrated Weekly*. The editors of the New York City magazine liked the picture and offered her a job as a "roving commissioner." This offer meant that, with the editor's approval, she could go anywhere she thought there was an interesting story. At that time journalists were beginning to recognize that photographs enhanced written articles and Sadie did both well.

A new reporter, she covered stories for *Leslie's* for sixteen years, from the end of the Spanish American War through World War I. She and other journalists helped *Leslie's Illustrated Weekly's* circulation go from 75,000 in 1900 to 380,000 in 1914 and she now signed all her stories, Mrs. Charles R. Miller, not S.K.M. Although this feminine lady was just five feet tall, she was quite outspoken and fearless in her pursuits. She seemed to know where the stories were and was often the first to "scoop" a story. National publications were quick to print her columns, which frustrated other journalists who were not as quick.

As a result of the success of the photograph taken at the Naval Academy, Sadie had a soft spot for sailors. She enjoyed a special camaraderie with midshipmen and they placed her photographs in the senior class's annual yearbook, the *Lucky Bag*. She photographed them often, and as a result, she became an unofficial public relations representative for the Academy. Because the school respected her professionalism, she was the only journalist the Navy allowed to photograph John Paul Jones's re-internment at the Academy's Chapel many years later.

She thought nothing of hauling fifty pounds of camera equipment when she was on assignment. In an article that Helen Buss Mitchell wrote for Baltimore's *News American*, she described an incident. As Sadie boarded a trolley car, a man offered to help her with her heavy cameras. After thanking him and exchanging introductions, he said that he knew a Charles Miller who was head of the Fidelity and Trust Company. Sadie replied that he was her husband. Somewhat perplexed because it seemed unlikely that a man in Charles Miller's position would allow his wife to work, the man said, "but you work." Her brown eyes twinkled with amusement as she responded, "Yes, and my husband beats me as well."[2]

While Charles was very proud of his wife and often traveled with her, Sadie was not afraid to travel alone. She believed that if one commanded respect, one received respect. But Sadie did not forget her domestic responsibilities if Charles did not accompany her. Before each trip she met with her household help and planned all of Charles's meals for the trip's duration. She would then know that he was eating well.

Early in her career, the editors of *Leslie's Weekly* sent her to Washington, DC, to take photographs at Indian Head proving grounds, where all the explosives for the country were made. It was off limits to the general public, but Sadie had the reputation of being discreet and government officials knew that she would photograph only what they allowed. When the editors saw her photographs, they said that the prints were dark and asked why she had not used a flash. Sadie curtly replied, "I was in a powder factory."[3]

Whether climbing Pike's Peak at 14,000 feet or descending into mines far below the earth's surface, Sadie carried her cameras and chased stories. In 1904 she crossed the Rocky Mountains in a railroad car, a brave journey for anyone at that time. The same year, when Baltimore's great fire broke out, Sadie took pictures from the roof of a fireproof building. The building's owner was surprised at her presence and asked, "How did you get up here? Sadie replied, "Well, I did not fall up the steps."[4] A few years later, she traveled by dogsled to the Yukon and panned for gold. During the trip she became stuck on ice for three days, which gave her time to take many photographs and write interesting accounts of her experiences. She sent these photo essays, including, "With the Camera in the Yukon," to *Leslie's* and foreign newspapers later published them as well.

In the early 1900s, the women's suffrage movement became newsworthy and Sadie covered their conventions. When Baltimore hosted the movement's national convention in 1906, Sadie was there and photographed Susan B. Anthony. It was the last photograph taken of the famous suffrage leader before her death. The suffragettes asked her why she signed her articles Mrs. Charles R. Miller rather than Sadie Kneller Miller. Wasn't she proud of using her own name? "Yes, but I am also proud to have a husband,"[5] she answered.

In April of the same year, Sadie went to San Francisco to photograph the damage left by an earthquake and the resulting fire that nearly destroyed the city. Later, undaunted by possible dangers, she went to the Caribbean and reported on the devastation left by an earthquake in Jamaica and a revolution in Haiti. She was in Cuba when sailors raised the *Maine*, the naval ship that had been sunk during the Spanish American War and she boarded the rising ship, determined to get a picture of its engine room. The sailors were so impressed when they saw her sliding through the mud to get her photographs that they wanted their pictures taken with the fearless reporter. When friends expressed concern over her dangerous destinations, Sadie replied that she loved adventure and that the magazine editors did not force her to go to places where she might be harmed.

During her career at *Leslie's Weekly,* the magazine sent her to cover five national presidential conventions. The editors made sure that she had her own entry badge and other privileges so that no one would interfere with her work. This was a first for a woman. Sadie felt that it was her duty to provide the most accurate information for the magazine's readers and at one convention she even climbed a telephone pole in order to capture a panoramic scene of the delegates below.

People had long wanted a way to shorten shipping times between the Atlantic and Pacific oceans. Creating a canal on the isthmus between South and North America would eliminate ships going around Cape Horn. When the Panama Canal was under construction, Sadie once again hoisted her skirts and climbed one hundred feet up to a construction site where she could best photograph the excavation. She visited the Canal site several times to report on its progress and newspapers from all over the country featured her photographs.

In 1907 Baltimore had just completed phase one of its sewer system and city leaders were anxious to show it off. Sadie joined other officials and later filed a hilarious story in the *Baltimore Sun* titled, "Woman's Trip through Baltimore's New Sewers in an Automobile." She wrote of how she and five prominent men from Baltimore arrived at the opening of the sewer in a large touring car. She described entering the sewer, whose diameter was twelve feet, just large enough for the car, and how they drove six miles through a serpentine tunnel only to find it necessary to stop when the tunnel became too narrow to go further. Because there was no room to turn around, the only way out was to back out. The tunnel was dark and it was difficult to see the curves. When something sharp punctured a wheel, Sadie brought out her camera so that its light might help the men to see while they changed the tire. Four hours later they returned to where they began.

People could recognize the young journalist by her dress. She consistently wore brown in the winter and white in the summer regardless of where she was. She traveled to every state, to every important city, and on every railroad from Mexico to Canada. For Sadie the story came first, regardless of personal inconvenience. At the end of the Republican Convention in 1908, when they nominated William Taft, a blizzard delayed her return to New York City. Concerned that her column might not make the deadline, she called the editors at *Leslie's*. They delayed printing the next day's journal until Sadie arrived. Not stopping for food or rest, Sadie developed her pictures and the magazine went to press. Once again, Sadie had "scooped" a story.

She filed illustrated stories from a leper colony in Hawaii and from cholera camps in Russia. When Spain fought for control of Morocco in 1911, Sadie took pictures from the front lines of artillery fire in Melilla. Everyone in the war-stricken town noticed Sadie, for she was the only white woman and she was dressed in summertime white. Furthermore, she photographed as close to gunfire as physically possible. Her peers were amazed by her courage and they praised her excellent writing and photography. Newspapers now referred to her as the first woman war correspondent and she became a prominent member of the League of American Presswomen.

At the beginning of World War I, Charles accompanied Sadie to Helgoland, an island in the North Sea held by the Germans. Sadie was taking pictures of the German artillery and ships when a German soldier stopped them and accused the Millers of being English spies. Charles told them they were American tourists and provided proof of their American citizenship. Eventually, the Germans released them, but not before a German officer confiscated the film in Sadie's camera. But Sadie had tricked him. She had just put new film in the camera and there were no photographs on it. Sadie sent her pictures to government officials in the United States.

She photographed many important people such as President Theodore Roosevelt, Jerome Bonaparte, and Alice Roosevelt Longworth. Unusual things also caught her interest. She took pictures of the Supreme Court's Bible at the time of Roosevelt's inauguration because it had had ten covers kissed off over the years. She took pictures of Abraham Lincoln's Bible and the first book of the Treasury Department. She went to Boston to take a picture of a petition to save *Old Ironsides* because it contained 30,000 names.

Sadie ignored protocol if she wanted a story. When Prince Louis of Battenberg came to the United States, Sadie decided not to wait for an invitation to speak with him but she hired her own launch and went out to his ship. Speechless at her audacity, but charmed by her personality, the Prince posed for pictures and then sent her back to shore on his private launch.

One of her more famous stories was her interview with Pancho Villa in 1912. Many reporters were anxious to talk to the colorful Mexican revolutionist, but Sadie beat them to the story. With her usual boldness, she hired a taxi, filled it with her equipment, and drove across the Mexican border to the terrorist's hideout in the mountains. Pancho Villa welcomed her into his retreat and proceeded to show her around. He proudly wore expensive jewelry that he had stolen for his wife from a Texas jewelry store just a week before. Sadie found him to be a polite host but just a few weeks later he shot several men in cold blood.

Although Sadie traveled the world for photojournalistic stories, she never ignored Maryland. Readers of *Leslie's Illustrated Weekly* often enjoyed descriptions of crab feasts on Maryland's Eastern Shore, society ladies shopping at Lexington Market, rural mail delivery, and her favorite topic, Naval Academy Midshipmen.

Toward the end of her career, she was riding in a hansom cab in New York City when it was struck by a trolley car. The driver was hurt but Sadie was not. As she walked away from the accident she realized that she had left her luggage and returned to get it. A policeman stopped her and asked if she saw the accident. Sadie curtly replied that she was the accident.

The Millers' house became a showpiece as a result of the items Sadie brought home from her many travels for *Leslie's*. She gave each room a theme and in 1911 the *Baltimore American* wrote an article about the Millers' home, including photographs, titled, "An Artistic Woman's Unique Home." The library reflected Sadie's appreciation for Native American crafts, which she saw when on assignment in the Southwest. Beneath a red and green ceiling Navaho rugs lay on top of dark hardwood floors. Green burlap covered the walls and draperies and pillows made from cloth woven by Navajo Indians highlighted the room's decor. The formal parlor contained mahogany furniture and the ceiling was gold satin. The music room housed items from Germany and was painted green, as was the dining room, which they called the Colonial Room. In that room traditional mahogany furniture that the couple received as wedding gifts was set beneath a ceiling of elaborate friezes. The main bedroom was papered in silk stripes and its massive furniture was made of golden oak. Pink silk draperies decorated the windows and there were mirrored doors. Sadie called it the Marie Antoinette Room. The kitchen was up to date and even had a laundry room. Sadie insisted on having light fixtures and telephones all over the house, even though few people had them at the time. There was an electric light on the front porch and Sadie's personally designed house number was readily apparent to all visitors.

In 1920 Sadie Miller died at the age of 52 from complications due to a stroke. Sadly, little more was known of Sadie's life. She might have been completely forgotten if Professor Keith Richwine of Western Maryland College had not pursued her history. He knew of Sadie's reputation and that she was an alumna of the school. But there was little information about her. He took time off from teaching to research records at the Enoch Pratt Library and anywhere else he could find information about this intriguing young lady. Unfortunately, there was no personal correspondence or records of her business transactions. After Sadie died, Charles Miller remarried. For whatever reason, all of Sadie's belongings, as well as her personal letters, were discarded. Although the house where Sadie grew up in Westminster still stands, little more could be learned about the family and all records from *Leslie's Weekly Illustrated* were destroyed when its office building caught fire shortly after Sadie's death.

In the 1980s Professor Richwine put together an exhibit of Sadie's photographs, which he found in old copies of *Leslie's Weekly*. He obtained other images from a distant niece. He successfully campaigned to have Sadie elected into Maryland's Women Hall of Fame posthumously in 1988. Without his interest and research, we would not know about this feisty, accomplished woman, who many consider the most adventurous photojournalist of her time.

Alta Schrock, 1911-2001
Community Activist

Alta Schrock

Alta Schrock was a rather frail child and seemed a bit bashful. At ease with her sisters and brothers, she did not seek out the company of others and preferred being outdoors, often by herself. She would become an energetic and courageous woman whose vision, determination, and faith would lead the people of her beloved Allegheny Mountain region to celebrate their culture and support themselves.

She was born on April 3, 1911, at Strawberry Hill Farm, one mile north of Grantsville, Maryland. She was the oldest of Alvin and Amelia Schrock's eight children. While her family did not have much in the way of material goods, they were comfortable with their lives and shared a strong belief in the Mennonite faith, which emphasized simplicity, nonviolence, and the importance of taking care of others. For several years her father operated a gristmill in Pennsylvania, but when his uncle died, he returned to Maryland to run the family farm for his aunt. Alta was seven years old when they moved to the farm, and she was delighted to be living there. Years later she treasured the memory of the two apple orchards her grandfather had planted, the sound of the wind in the Norway spruce, the sugar maple grove, and the brook that ran through the hemlock forest. She would help with the work in the washhouse and the milking-shed, and loved to watch the swallows building their nests in the loft of the pigpen. Paths in her grandmother's vegetable garden were lined with chamomile, pansies edged the kitchen porch, and peonies, bleeding heart, and sweet-smelling flowering currant gave color to the broad lawn. Childhood at Strawberry Hill taught her to take joy in the natural world and to take care of it.

The family lived simply and had little money to spend. Reading was one of their favorite activities and the children practiced memorizing verses from the Bible and poems, and then reciting to the others. While the Schrock children did not have a lot of things, they did have the whole outdoor world all around the house, and they were out and about in the woods whenever they could be. They often went on picnics and regularly went to church together on Sundays. Sometimes, on the way home, their father would stop the car and tell his children to be quiet and to roll down the windows and listen. With no voices to get in the way, the sounds and scents of the natural world were clear. Like her parents, Alta loved nature, and whenever her mother did not need her to help with daily household chores—and sometimes when she did—the young girl was apt to be busy investigating plants in the woods in back of the house or watching the swallows or the farm animals. Her mother always knew she could find Alta outdoors.

Alta was not a strong or vigorous youngster. The cause of her illness or weakness is unclear, but she needed the help of a younger sister to walk to and from the local elementary school. Some accounts describe her as being rather shy during that time. Her sister Ada did not completely agree with that judgment, but did say Alta was not a pushy or noisy youngster. It was not the usual local Mennonite custom to continue studies past the grade school level, so once she finished seventh grade, Alta stayed home.

This was a stroke of luck. Alta was blessed with plenty of curiosity, and the outdoors became her laboratory. There was a small cabin in the woods behind the house. One story is that Alta's father built it for her; another story claims that Alta herself built it using lumber given to her father to settle a debt. However it happened, the cabin was her refuge. She lugged a heavy typewriter to it. Then, after she spent many hours observing in the woods and fields, she would go to the cabin and type up what she had discovered. Bit by bit she taught herself about the woods she loved, with a special emphasis on botany. Once she assembled a collection of 300 medicinal plants, entered the collection in a local contest, and won a twenty dollar gold piece!

As time went on, this program of self-study was not enough. She was ready for more formal education, and at the urging of a relative, she returned to school at age seventeen. She seemed to have overcome her earlier illness, for now she walked four miles each way to attend high school. Her science teacher was so impressed with her knowledge and her ability to learn that he allowed her to work late in the laboratory and trusted her to lock it securely when she left for the night. One night, after she had returned home, she could not remember whether or not she had locked the laboratory door. She returned to the school on horseback, accompanied by two cousins, to find that she had indeed locked the door and could go home with an easy conscience. Late in her senior year, she had to drop out because of poor health. As she began to feel a little better, she continued to wander in the fields and woods of the area and study the plants and flowers. Family friends recommended her to a young woman student who needed help assembling a collection of wildflowers for a school project. The woman's teacher, a professor of botany at Waynesburg College and its president as well, was so impressed with the collection and with Alta, that he offered her a scholarship to the college.

Throughout her life her curiosity helped make her an exceptional learner, and she knew she wanted to go to college. But this was the time of the Great Depression. Although she had a scholarship, which would pay for her classes, she had no money for a room to live in or for the books she would need. Her father had a feed business, but many of his customers could not pay the money they owed his store. She was determined to keep trying, and began canning food and remaking used clothing. Help came from unexpected places. During her high school years she had written a weekly nature column for the local newspaper, *The Meyersdale Republican*. This undertaking would later benefit her. A couple who had lived in the area but had moved to Kansas heard Alta needed money for school. They had enjoyed the columns she wrote in the *Republican* and were impressed with her knowledge. One week while Alta was puzzling over her money problems, a letter arrived from the woman in Kansas. Along with a note she sent a check for $50 to help with college costs, and she asked Alta not to tell her husband, since he might not understand. The next week a second letter arrived from Kansas. This one, from the woman's husband, held a check for $100 and a note asking Alta not to tell his wife. The letters swept away all her doubts: somehow she would go to college.

Lack of money was a problem throughout her years in college. Each summer she returned home and worked with determination to grow food. She canned everything she could and took it back to school with her in the fall. At times she had as little as fifteen cents a week to add fresh things to her diet of home-canned rations and occasionally she did not know where her next meal would come from. Yet each time there was a crisis, somehow help turned up. Once, without having talked with her, Alta's parents simply turned up at the college with a car full of canned fruits and vegetables, most of which she ate, some of which she sold. Once a man who had once been fifty cents short when he bought vegetables from her ran into Alta on the street and gave that fifty cents to her. In later years Alta trusted that if money was needed it would appear. Where it came from might be a surprise, but she was confident that it would turn up.

Poor health troubled her again in the winter of 1935-1936. She was in the hospital for a week, and then went home to recuperate. With her she brought the bill from the hospital. As a student she was charged very little, but even the small $25 fee was too much for her. She did not have the money. Alta fretted about the bill and looked for ways to pay it. At last she came up with an idea, which she shared with one of her cousins: she envisioned the grounds of Dr. Springer's Health Retreat landscaped with native trees and shrubs. Her cousin urged her to take her plan to Dr. Springer himself. Alta was nervous and very unsure of herself, but she did what her cousin suggested, took a deep breath, and presented her ideas directly to Dr. Springer. She was delighted when he agreed with her plan and even more pleased when he hired a helper to assist with the heavy work of digging and planting all those trees and shrubs. Best of all, the doctor paid her $25 for her week's work—exactly the amount of money she owed the hospital. Now she could pay her debt.

She graduated from Waynesburg with an A.B. degree in biology in 1937 and continued studying, finally earning her Ph.D. from the University of Pittsburgh in 1944. Money was always a concern, but she was becoming more confident that she could cope with financial difficulties. When she first came to Pittsburgh she struggled to find a room for rent within walking distance of the campus, and finally found one on the third floor of a house on Bellefield Avenue. Her brother made her a folding table, and she cooked on a one-burner hot plate. She washed her few dishes in the bathroom. The room was private and peaceful, a fine place for studying. Her financial situation was improving. She earned $50 a month as a graduate assistant to the head of the biology department. She sent half of her salary to a sister who was studying at Goshen College and gave $20 to her landlady. This left her $5 for her own expenses. To earn more income, she baby-sat, sold handicrafts, and washed dishes for local organizations' dinners and banquets. Those jobs offered her an important bonus, for she was sometimes given delicious leftovers to carry home. On weekends she was often hired to be a tour guide for groups visiting the Carnegie Museum. In addition to working odd jobs, Alta liked to watch the Pittsburgh Symphony performances, which she saw from the cheapest seats; she also made friends at the Presbyterian Church. Alta struggled to earn her education, and she met the challenges she was given head-on and learned from them.

After receiving her Ph.D. she taught biology at American University in Washington, DC, for two years, and then taught at both Bluffton and Goshen Colleges in Indiana. When she had first enrolled at Waynesburg she took stock of herself; she had few close friends, and set herself to work toward meeting and becoming friends with more people. When she went to Goshen she bought and renovated an old hay barn, which she named "Fliederhof," and it was a haven for her students. They came to talk, listen, and share their stories by the fireside. A pot of fragrant tea was always ready on the stove. Alta's childhood shyness disappeared as she made a comfortable and welcoming place for students to gather for casual or serious conversation or a chance to enjoy informal singing together. Students were at ease at Fliederhof and at least one group took to the meadow outside to perform their version of *Peter and the Wolf.*

Her caring for others went beyond looking after her students. She saw to it that three of her younger sisters had a chance to go to college, and during World War II she served as a practical nurse in Civilian Public Service Camps. Later she helped Mennonite refugees with their paperwork and resettlement when they came to live in the United States. After the war, she went to Germany where she worked as the coordinator of a neighborhood center in Berlin. She was able to do some traveling in that country, and as always she was interested in everything she saw. One thing she noticed was that many people worked with handicrafts, such as woodworking, sewing, and other crafts for the home. She noted, too, that those craftspeople worked together to organize the sale of their goods, and that as they did the sales increased. Alta would remember this and use the information later in a project of her own.

Although her teaching responsibilities, as well as her relief work after the war kept her busy, Alta always kept close ties to her beloved Allegheny region and when she came home for a visit she continued to learn about the people of the area and their ways and their history. She was fascinated by what she discovered. The mountain residents were often independent, poor, and proud. Their family histories were full of local folklore and their households, while modest, held many examples of their woodworking, weaving, and other crafts they made. The people of the Allegheny highlands were often shy and were not at ease with outsiders. Alta, once shy herself, was becoming a persistent and cheerful visitor in their homes. She always drove a green car and when people saw it coming they knew it was Alta Schrock, not a stranger, approaching.

Finally, her love for the people and the Allegheny countryside drew her away from Indiana. She felt called to return to the region, and she took a job as a professor of biology at Frostburg State University in Garrett County. Alta was home and she was ready to work. Her sister Ada, drawing on words from a traditional prayer, described Alta as a "possibility thinker," and it was Alta's ability to think imaginatively about problems that would build her legacy. She was concerned about the living conditions of the rural families. Poverty was everywhere. Many households had little income; some people were unable to work at all. Further, their rich culture was in danger of disappearing. Alta saw this as a challenge, and she loved challenges. She traveled through the region looking for spinners, weavers, potters, quilters, and other craft artists, and encouraged them to keep practicing their skills. As she had since childhood, she kept careful and detailed notes of what she learned. When they needed help with equipment, she searched for and found such things as looms, spinning wheels, potters wheels, or sewing machines, and had them put in working order. Then, in her green car, she delivered that equipment to wherever it was needed. Her energy and support were encouraging to the artisans.

Next, in a building along Route 40, National Road, she founded Penn Alps. This would be an outlet where the crafts they produced could be sold and where their culture would be celebrated. Today the building houses a restaurant well-known for its home-cooked meals and a shop filled with pottery, quilts, carved wooden bowls, as well as beautiful shawls, table linens, blankets, and all sorts of other crafts. A generous section of the shop is devoted to local history as well. Providing necessary extra income for the people in the region was one of Alta's original goals, and the shop was a vehicle generating revenue. On the opposite side of the parking lot she built Spruce Forest Artisan Village. This area contained several restored cabins that served as studios where artists could stay and work between May and December. Artists such as wood carvers, chair caners, rug braiders, and other craftsmen were invited to stay for a month, and they were happy to talk with visitors and explain their work. This served a second goal, that of education. One of the cabins in this section was Alta's own cabin from her childhood.

In addition to Penn Alps and Spruce Forest Artisan Village, Alta was a founder of the Springs, Pennsylvania, Historical Society, the Springs Folk Festival, the Mennonite Youth Village for Underprivileged Children, Garrett County Community Action, Inc., and the Tri-State Council of the Alleghenies. She served as editor and a frequent writer for *The Casselman Chronicles*. This collection of stories from the Casselman Valley included articles as diverse as the making of rennet cheese, different types of cowbells, the history of the Mason Dixon Line, the geology of a local mountain, and family stories and obituaries of residents. She also edited the annual *Journal of the Alleghenies*. She remained a faithful member of the Mennonite Church throughout her life and her belief made her strong in spirit. In her later years, she maintained her physical strength by exercising daily on her trampoline; she did not do stunts, her sister Ada explained, she simply jumped.

Persuasive and secure in her work, and blessed with a positive outlook, Alta Schrock brought significant changes to her beloved mountains. Yet in almost every photograph she is either smiling or on the edge of a smile; in spite of the difficulties she faced in making her dreams for others come true, she does not seem to be worried or concerned that her dreams might not work to her satisfaction. This quiet, frail child grew into a confident dreamer who became a mover of mountains.

Helen Brooke Taussig, 1898-1986
Pediatric Cardiologist

Helen Taussig was born and raised in Cambridge, Massachusetts. The family lived near Harvard University, where Helen's father, Frank William Taussig, taught economics. People all across the country considered him an outstanding economist and students flocked to his classes. Her mother, Edith Guild Taussig, loved biology and botany, which she studied at Radcliffe College, later part of Harvard University. Helen was the youngest of four children. They all received excellent educations and participated in a wide variety of activities. But there were challenges ahead for the future pediatric cardiologist. From those challenges, Helen would learn the values of perseverance, compassion, and maintaining a positive attitude.

Helen was bright and inquisitive. When her parents invited guests for dinner, their youngest daughter enjoyed listening to the conversation and often asked questions. When she was not studying or playing sports, she could be found working with her father tending his garden. She spent hours with a magnifying glass, examining the pistils and stamens of flowers, teaching herself the process of fertilization. Sowing seeds and watching them sprout became a lifelong interest. For the rest of her life, wherever she lived, she would have a garden.

Summertime found the family in Cotuit, a town on Cape Cod, where they owned a rambling house with wraparound porches that overlooked the water. Although summer activities beckoned, the Taussigs insisted that their children study each morning. They learned German from their father and botany from their mother. Professor Taussig, an accomplished violinist, taught the children to appreciate music. They spent the afternoons swimming, sailing, and playing tennis, and Helen excelled in them all, especially tennis. However, there was one area in which she did not do well. Helen could not read. To her, letters appeared backwards and words and numbers flipped and rearranged themselves. She remembered awful times when she was called on to read aloud in class. She stumbled over words and her teachers thought she was lazy and ridiculed her. Helen had dyslexia, a reading disorder that was unknown at the time. Her mother did her best to help her, but when Helen was eleven her mother died from tuberculosis and from then on her father took over and helped her with her reading and spelling. He tutored his daughter with a sense of humor and great patience.

Helen too, developed tuberculosis soon after her mother died. Fortunately, it was a mild case but it did interrupt her schooling and reading progress. The doctors allowed Helen to attend classes only in the mornings and ordered her to rest in the afternoons. They recommended that she get as much fresh air as possible, which at that time was a common prescription for those with the disease. Helen began sleeping on the porch, something she continued to do for the rest of her life. Later she reminisced about this time as one that taught her to be patient towards those with limited physical abilities and to save her strength for important things.

By the time Helen entered ninth grade at the Cambridge School for Girls, she could manage her reading assignments and she earned respectable grades. Reading became easier as she went through high school. But reading for pleasure would never become a favorite pastime.

She attended Radcliffe College for two years. Although she did all right academically and was involved with the school's extracurricular activities, she asked her father to allow her to transfer to the University of California at Berkeley. At Radcliffe everyone knew her as Professor Taussig's daughter and she wanted to become more independent. Also, he had recently remarried and it seemed like a good time to try something new. She had visited Berkeley when her father taught a course there the previous summer and liked what she saw. At Berkeley, along with her studies, she enjoyed many of the same activities that she had at Harvard. She continued to play championship tennis, and kept up an interest in the theater. Berkeley's surrounding areas provided many hiking paths, another favorite pastime. When she graduated from Berkeley in 1921 the question was, what did she want to do?

She had thought about medicine as a career but she knew it was a difficult path for women. Men dominated the field and many people thought that women were too delicate and should not have to see the workings of the human body. In 1921 only about 6% of the doctors in the United States were female and they usually received their degrees in Europe or at all-women medical schools in the United States. Her father suggested that she consider the field of public health. Harvard had just opened a School of Public Health and Helen made an appointment to talk with the dean. He told her that she could study medicine for two years but that she would not be accepted as a candidate for a medical degree. Helen asked him why anyone would do that. Certainly not she! The discussion removed any uncertainties that Helen had about her career. She was going to be a doctor.

Once she had made this decision she set about taking the courses she would need to enter medical school. Harvard allowed women to take a few courses as special students and Helen enrolled in a class in histology, the study of the body's tissues. She was the only woman in the class, had to sit apart from the men so she would not "contaminate" them, and was not allowed to conduct lab experiments with them. Recognizing Helen's ability, her histology professor urged her not to waste time taking courses at Harvard, where she would never receive credit, but to transfer to Boston University, where she would. She took his advice and studied anatomy under Dr. Alexander Begg at Boston. He immediately recognized the capabilities of this young woman and suggested that she study heart muscles. Dissecting cow hearts and learning how muscles contracted captured her interest and she conducted an experiment showing how parts of animal heart muscles could be induced to mimic the heart's rhythm when submerged in a special solution. She wrote up the experiment and the *American Journal of Physiology* published her results in 1925. With Dr. Begg's support, she applied to Johns Hopkins Medical School, which had been admitting women since 1893.

Helen was accepted and worked in the pediatric heart clinic while she was a student at Hopkins. After graduating in 1927, she remained at the clinic as a fellow. When she did not receive a residency in internal medicine, she decided to concentrate on pediatrics and became an intern in the heart clinic. She caught the attention of the new head of pediatrics, Dr. Edwards A. Park, who became Helen's mentor and teacher. Dr. Park assigned department members to take charge of special areas, a decision he made based on their professional publications. When Helen joined the Hopkins faculty in 1930 he asked her to head the clinic.

Just as she was beginning her career, Helen began to lose her hearing. Doctors were not sure why, perhaps it was the result of a childhood case of whooping cough. This added a great deal of stress for the new pediatric cardiologist. How was she going to treat her young patients when she could not hear heartbeats with a stethoscope? How was she going to be able to talk with their parents?

She met the challenge by using hearing aids and by teaching herself to read lips, but both had limitations. Hearing aids were bulky and not very strong. She wore one beneath her clothes, and when she could not hear someone she pulled the device out and asked the person to talk directly into it. Lip reading was difficult—even more so than regular reading. Many words looked the same when spoken and names were especially hard. Very often she asked people to write down what they were saying. When attending lectures, she made sure to sit in the front row with her back toward the light so that she could see the speaker's lips. Listening to a young patient's heartbeat even using an amplified stethoscope was not satisfactory. As a result she taught herself to hear with her hands. With the radio playing she felt vibrations from music in the furniture cushions to see how they varied. When examining a baby she held her hand gently against the child's chest near the heart where she could feel the pulsations. Gentleness became her trademark. Other doctors were amazed when she detected heart murmurs or abnormal heartbeats when they had not heard them with the stethoscope.

She spent her summers on Cape Cod where she followed her childhood routine. She rose early, swam, and worked all morning. Afternoons were for relaxation. She loved to entertain, but there were rules. She told her guests they were on their own in the mornings for breakfast and activities, but that she would happily join them for lunch and afternoon fun. The group might play tennis, go sailing, or canoeing, or take long walks, always accompanied by one of Helen's dogs. Her guests often helped with meal preparations either shucking oysters or cleaning shrimp. Dinners included Helen's homemade bread that she baked nearly every week whether she was in Baltimore or on the Cape. Those summers allowed her to spend time with her sisters who also owned houses there. She relished the hours watching her nieces and nephews enjoying the same activities that she and her siblings had. But she was always glad to return to Baltimore in September.

Patients came to Harriet Lane from all over because it was known as one of the best clinics in the country for treating children with rheumatic fever. Before scientists discovered penicillin in 1928, rheumatic fever was the leading cause of death in children. Helen often wondered how the clinic could have handled the number of sick children if the drug did not exist.

At Dr. Park's insistence, she began to investigate heart malformations and heart abnormalities that were present at birth. Frightened parents came to the clinic when their children showed symptoms of bluish skin (hence the term "blue babies") and labored breathing. The children had a serious condition known as cyanosis, which occurred when blood was not properly oxygenated due to deformities in all four valves of the heart. Helen spent long hours with these young patients and felt that there had to be a surgical procedure to help them. But who dared to operate on a young child's beating heart? It was unheard of.

Helen became one of the first doctors to diagnose heart problems using two new visual instruments and she was eager for colleagues to follow her lead. Physicians from all over the world applied for a one-year fellowship program to study under Helen. They crammed into a small room at the hospital, which contained the fluoroscope. This machine passed x-ray beams through the patient's body, which then projected an image of the patient's heart onto a fluorescent screen. Looking at the heart from different angles allowed doctors to actually see the heart beating, see existing abnormalities, and evaluate heart rhythms. This had never been possible. The second instrument was the electrocardiograph, which made graphic records of heartbeats. Unfortunately, many of the children brought to the clinic were very sick and died. Helen attended every autopsy in order to learn more about heart abnormalities. She traveled often to meet with other doctors who were beginning to explore this medical frontier. She was determined to find a way to save cyanotic patients.

As she gathered more information, she suspected that patients were not dying of heart failure, but because their blood did not receive enough oxygen. She was convinced that rerouting their blood flow would save their lives, but no one agreed with her. When Dr. Alfred Blalock became the chair of Hopkins' surgery department in 1941, Helen was eager to share her theory with him. The challenge intrigued him and he agreed to work with her. He and his surgical assistant, Mr. Vivien Thomas, who came with him from Vanderbilt University, spent two years trying to solve the circulatory problems in blue babies. During this time Mr. Thomas operated on over 200 dogs to refine the procedure. The operation became successful, but who knew if it would work on humans?

In 1944 one of Helen's patients became critically ill. The child's parents agreed with Dr. Blalock that the only chance the baby had for survival was to undergo the new operation. Dr. William H. Zinkham, an intern at Hopkins at the time, and later a colleague of Dr. Taussig's, watched as Dr. Blalock, assisted by Dr. Henry Bahnson and the technical advice of Mr. Thomas, rerouted the patient's blood. Dr. Taussig walked around the operating table observing every aspect of the surgery. "There was high drama in the operating arena as everyone witnessed the child's face change from blue to pink,"[1] Dr. Zinkham said. After Dr. Blalock successfully operated on two more patients, he and Helen felt confident about the operation and wrote an article, "The Surgical Treatment of Malformations of the Heart," which was published in the *Journal of the American Medical Association* in 1947. Known as the Blalock-Taussig operation, doctors around the world began to perform it, saving many children's lives.

Years later a group protested the use of dogs in animal experiments. Dr. Taussig and a few of her colleagues met with the protesters and listened to their arguments. One physician pointed out that doctors would never have dared to perform the Blalock-Taussig procedure unless it had been tried on dogs first. After he introduced several surviving cyanotic patients, the protestors became quiet. In 1951 the Baltimore Animal Aid Association presented a plaque and a painting of Anna, the dog on which Dr. Blalock performed the first successful blue baby operation. The plaque stated, "For Service to Humanity Through Science." Helen loved dogs and owned many over the course of her life. She later testified before Congress in support of using animals in medical research.

The successful operation made the clinic world famous, and it received an overwhelming number of referrals. Although not every patient was a candidate for surgery, Helen herself recommended over a thousand patients for the procedure. She felt that it was her duty to teach as many young doctors as she could because the more doctors who could perform the operation, the more blue babies would live. These doctors proudly called themselves "the loyal Knights of Taussig." They enjoyed annual meetings at Helen's home either on the Cape or in Baltimore.

Some people considered Helen Taussig shy. But nothing stopped her from expressing an opinion if she disagreed with anything relating to her patients, and at times she and Dr. Blalock disagreed. But, her patients adored her; she was gentle, reassuring, and available. She never pressured families to have the operation, allowing them time to decide for themselves. One youngster recalled that after deciding to have the operation, Dr. Taussig told her she was looking forward to showing the young girl her post-operative fingers. They would be pink, not blue. When the youngster awoke, Helen was by her bedside holding up the child's pink fingers. Helen maintained an ongoing correspondence with her patients and their families. Many brought their wives, husbands, or young children to meet the woman who had saved their lives. Years later, she published a twenty-eight year follow-up of all the children who had been operated on at Hopkins between 1945 and 1951.

She wrote *Congenital Malformations of the Heart* in 1947. The book became the bible for those interested in this specialized field, especially for those unable to study at Hopkins, and it led many medical students to become pediatric cardiologists. One doctor recalled that he operated with the book in one hand and the scalpel in the other. Many physicians felt that without the book the course of pediatric cardiology might have been delayed or changed. A revised second edition was published in 1960. In 1962 Helen and six other doctors founded the Board of Pediatric Cardiology.

Over the years both she and Dr. Blalock traveled the world and spoke at many medical conventions. Aware of her limits in hearing her own voice, Helen had someone in the back of the room signal her if her voice level needed correction. Wherever she went, she was an eager learner. Even in her eighties, after she visited the Great Wall of China on a very cold day, a colleague remembered that she was very excited about all that she had seen. Her thirst for knowledge made her a good conversationalist and people looked forward to talking with her.

Among the many awards Helen received throughout her career were the French Chevalier d'Honneur, the Italian Feltrinelli Prize, the Peruvian Presidential Medal of Honor, the Albert Lasker Award for outstanding contributions to medicine, and the Elizabeth Blackwell Award, (given to women whose lives exemplified outstanding service to humanity). However, the awards did not make up for the gender disparities that existed in the medical field during these years. In 1945, when the National Academy of Sciences, one of medicine's most prestigious groups, elected Dr. Blalock to membership, it ignored Helen. When Dr. Blalock came to Hopkins, the university immediately promoted him to the rank of professor but it took sixteen years for the University to promote Helen to associate professor.

Despite the inequalities, she opposed the idea that medical schools should admit as many women as men, recognizing that many women would choose to raise families rather than practice medicine. However, she fought for women whenever she could. In 1956 she sat on the Pediatric Department's intern selection committee when it made decisions about whom to select for the following year's interns. As she watched her colleagues throw candidates' folders into different piles on the floor, she realized that this was some sort of ranking procedure. She promptly got down on her hands and knees and pushed the women's folders forward. Although there were few female medical students in those days, she wanted them to have a fair chance in the procedure. As the number of female students increased, Helen advised them not to worry so much about the gender inequalities. What was important was to do their best. In order to be treated equally, she said, they had to work just as hard as men. Certainly Helen Taussig did.

In 1960 the drug company Merrill wanted approval to sell the drug thalidomide in the United States. Doctors in Europe had prescribed it to pregnant women who had sleeping problems. Dr. Frances Kelsey, newly appointed to the Food and Drug Administration, heard reports of dangerous side effects from the drug and wanted more time before allowing its usage in this country. In 1962, during a dinner conversation with a visiting German doctor, Helen learned that in some European countries doctors were seeing many children born with deformities such as flipper like appendages instead of arms, missing ears, flattened faces, and missing or deformed legs. Helen felt compelled to investigate anything that dealt with children and abnormalities and with Hopkins' permission she took a leave of absence and flew to Germany. She met with doctors in Germany and Great Britain where similar cases occurred. Medical tests eliminated heredity as a factor. What caused these abnormalities? Was it a virus? Were they the result of some sort of pollution? Some doctors felt that they were the result of women taking thalidomide during early stages of their pregnancy. The answers from questionnaires that the mothers of these unfortunate children gave led Helen to believe that the drug was the cause. These findings validated Dr. Kelsey's concerns. After Helen testified before the Senate, the Food and Drug Administration banned the sale of thalidomide in the United States. President John Kennedy gave Frances Kelsey the President's Medal for Distinguished Service in 1962 for her part in protecting Americans. Helen gave speeches and wrote many articles to make people aware of the dangers of the drug. She published her findings in *Scientific American* and *Journal of the American Medical Association,* and she wrote an editorial, "Dangerous Tranquility," for *Science* magazine. The work of both women helped prevent a similar crisis in the United States.

Helen Taussig retired from The Johns Hopkins Medical School in 1963, but accolades continued for the pioneering woman doctor. Seventeen universities around the world, including Harvard, awarded her honorary Doctor of Science degrees and in 1964 she received the Medal of Freedom from President Lyndon Johnson. In 1965 the American Heart Association elected her president of its organization, making her the first woman to hold that position. The election was significant because most of its members were internists and for them to recognize a female pediatrician was unusual. In 1972 the American College of Physicians named her "master," its highest honor, and again she was the first woman to receive that rank. In 1973 she was among the first group of women to be inducted into Maryland's Women Hall of Fame. In 1974 Johns Hopkins dedicated its cardiology division of the Children's Center to this fine woman who overcame many obstacles to become one of the most respected doctors in the world. The Helen B. Taussig Children's Cardiac Center sees over 5000 patients each year. Helen Taussig died in an automobile accident in 1986.

Mary Lemist Titcomb, 1852-1932

Librarian

The first bookmobile

Mary Lemist Titcomb was born in May 1852, in the small town of Farmington, New Hampshire. When she was very young, her family moved to the town of Exeter, where her brothers attended the Exeter School. Mary and her sister were taught at home by their mother for several years and then attended the Robinson Female Seminary. Neither girl was outgoing and Mary was described as a "...shy, timid girl, easily frightened into being almost panicky when forced into speech and action by the even greater timidity of her sister." But this fearful child would become a confident, self-assured woman, one of the most celebrated citizens of Washington County, Maryland, and her vision and determination would revolutionize public libraries all over the United States.

Once Mary finished school she did not take a job. There was no financial need for her to work. Like most young women who came from families like hers, she simply continued to live comfortably with her family in Exeter. It seemed an ordinary way of life. Yet Mary was not an ordinary woman. As time went by, her brothers married and were busy with their own families, and after the death of her father, Mary decided she wanted something more to do. Helping sick people would be an acceptable occupation, and she thought briefly about nursing, but did not seem to find it exciting. Then one Sunday she happened to read an article about librarianship in her church newsletter. She had always loved books and now she had found her career.

There was no school or formal training program nearby, so Mary set out to teach herself how to be a librarian. First she went to the nearby town of Concord and worked in its library as an unpaid volunteer. Her next job took her to Vermont, where she became a cataloguer at the Rutland Free Library. After she learned to inventory and classify books she was appointed its chief librarian. Her knowledge of how libraries operated was growing.

The state of Vermont's Library Commission asked Mary to join their group. She agreed and soon became its secretary. This once "timid girl" was one of only two women to hold a statewide office. Working as a library organizer, she traveled all over the state helping new and established libraries organize and arrange their books for the benefit of their communities. She was becoming more and more familiar with the ways different libraries operated, the things they all had in common, and the things that made each library unique.

During this time, while Mary traveled to many different areas of Vermont, leaders in Washington County, Maryland, came to a decisive and exciting decision: local leaders voted to build a public library. Hagerstown, where the library would be built, was an established and settled area, but most of the 500-square-mile county was farmland. There were no public high schools there and many people were either completely illiterate or had very little skill with reading. Even bustling Hagerstown lacked a bookstore.

When the announcement of the new library was made, people were pleased. They looked forward to having a building devoted to books in their community, they were sure the job of librarian would be given to someone who lived in town, and they knew that person would be happy to earn the librarian's $1,000 per year salary. So, when the library's founders announced that Mary Lemist Titcomb, a complete stranger who lived in New England, would be the chief librarian, they were indignant. Mary's vision for the library impressed community leaders, but her appointment caused an uproar among the general public. When she moved to town, some people claimed her manner was frosty, and they disliked what they called her "New England manner." Now many hundreds of miles from her comfortable family home in New Hampshire, shy Mary Titcomb had a challenge on her hands.

She began work on February 1, 1901. Her job was to make the library popular and to see that it was useful to the entire community. First, though, libraries needed books and Mary set about collecting them. Many were donated by townspeople. Some of those books were in poor shape and had to be thrown away, some she sent to a bindery for repairs, and a few were in good enough condition to go right on the shelves. With these donations, plus some individual gifts of books, she was able to classify and catalogue approximately 1700 volumes.

Once its books were in place, the Washington County Free Library opened its doors on August 1, 1901. The building was not quite finished and there was no formal ceremony. The founders simply put an announcement in the newspaper and hoped people would come. They did. An account of the day said people crowded into the building, eager to join the library. Even the president of the board, Edward Mealey, spent several hours at the main desk helping people register. The library's first day was a wonderful success.

Mary would not be satisfied just lending books to people who came to the building. She was determined to take the enthusiasm of the building's opening day, turn that excitement into a steady business, and then she wanted to reach out to the areas outside of Hagerstown and help those people learn the value of the library. She knew that to make the library an important part of the community, she must get to know the community herself. She quickly made herself at home in Hagerstown. She joined the Historical Society and the Civic League, was a member of the Current Events Club and the King's Daughters, and she attended St. John's Episcopal Church. She liked to know what was going on, and she made sure to be tactful in dealing with others. For example, when the question of women's suffrage came up, Mary said that while she was not a suffragist, she was confident that women would win the right to vote. When that happened, she, as a good citizen, would exercise that right.

The approximately 25,000 residents of Hagerstown appreciated and enjoyed their new library. A scrubwoman, who was one of its earliest customers, was very pleased that even residents from the poorest areas could borrow handsome new books, and a teenager, returning a Shakespeare play he had borrowed, gave the writer his seal of approval and announced he would like to read something else by the same man. To make sure the initial enthusiasm for the library continued, Mary quickly hired a children's librarian to look out for the youngest customers and she hired two more assistants the following year. Ms. Nellie Chrissinger began as an apprentice, advanced to paid work as a substitute at ten cents an hour in 1902, and became an assistant, whose responsibilities included training apprentices in April 1903.

A typical library was a building filled with orderly collections of books, but Mary Titcomb's Library would not be typical. She was determined that it would become an important part of the entire county, not just the city of Hagerstown. Most of the people who lived outside the city were farmers. They traveled by horse and buggy, and their travels did not take them into town very often. They had no contact with the library and Mary set out to change that. If she could not bring all those people to the library for books, she said, she would take the books to them. Drawing on the ideas of Melvil Dewey and other library experts, she started a "Boxes for Books" program. First, Mary and her assistants filled boxes with about 50 carefully chosen books from the library. Then she hired a horse and wagon, and asked the library janitor, Joshua Thomas, to deliver those boxes to certain places, called "stations," throughout the county. The stations were usually the general stores or post offices in rural communities, places where local people came fairly regularly.

Mr. Thomas, a native of Washington County, was a Civil War veteran. When he returned home after the war, he made a living by driving all over the county buying up butter, eggs, and country produce and taking those things to the market in Hagerstown. He learned the ins and outs of the county roads and he came to know the people as well. He was the perfect ambassador for the library. During the first year of the "Boxes for Books" program, there were 21 stations, and by 1904 there were 66. With Joshua Thomas as its agent, the program thrived. It was clear that some farm families who could not come to the library building in Hagerstown were enjoying books and were beginning to develop the habit of reading.

"Some" was not enough. Mary Titcomb wanted to reach many people, not just those who could or would take time to stop at the local general store or post office and see a very limited number of books. The boxes program was a start, and a successful one, but she knew that as the wagon traveled from one station to another, it passed many farms whose residents did not come to the books. It would be much better to bring the magic of books directly to people in their homes. The fact that this had not been done before did not trouble her.

Ms. Titcomb went to the library board and emphasized several points. First, a "library wagon," she said, would be a visible symbol of the Washington County Library and would be a friendly ambassador in rural areas. While the hired horse and wagon for the boxes program were satisfactory, a specially built wagon could hold many more books and could take those books directly to the borrowers. In addition, once the wagon was purchased, its upkeep would be reasonable, she pointed out. Finally, in Joshua Thomas they already had an experienced country driver, and the entire library staff was enthusiastic about the idea. The board agreed, and Mary drew up plans and interviewed wagon makers. The bookmobile was born.

The first book wagon had a distinctly boxy look. Painted a dull black with small, plain lettering, finished shelves inside held the books. Driven by Mr. Thomas and pulled by two horses, it frightened a number of people who thought it was a hearse. It certainly looked like one. An uneasy farmer, seeing the wagon coming into his yard, yelled that there were no dead people at his house. But Joshua Thomas drove into the yard anyway, greeted the farmer and his family cheerfully, and was soon a regular visitor. Other families were clearly suspicious of this newfangled idea. When the wagon drove into their yards they might open the door, but just a crack. When Mr. Thomas reported this after the book wagon's first run on April 1, 1905, Ms. Titcomb had the wagon's wheels and door panel painted red. It would never again be mistaken for the "dead wagon."

The book wagon was a success. It stopped at individual houses and gave people a chance both to choose their own books and to tell the driver of other books, or types of books, that they would like to read. It followed sixteen routes through the county's 500 square miles and took four days to complete a round trip. When Mary Titcomb was asked to address the American Library Association Conference at Bretton Woods in 1909, she was pleased to tell her audience that in Washington County people did not have to come to the books, for the books would come to them. Her dream was thriving.

That dream would be interrupted. "Smashed in a Railroad Wreck!" read the headline in *The Hagerstown Morning Herald* on August 25, 1910. As he approached a section of the Norfolk and Western Railroad track that day, Joshua Thomas did not have a clear view of the tracks because of the trees, and the noise of his wagon wheels drowned out the rumble of an approaching train. As the wagon crossed the tracks, it was struck. Mr. Thomas was thrown 20 feet, broke a rib, and suffered several cuts. The horses broke free and ran down the road a distance before they were caught, but they were not hurt. Books were scattered all over the ground, and the wagon itself was destroyed. Book wagon service was suspended through 1911.

There was no question that the program would continue, but it would change dramatically after the accident. Using a $2500 gift from the board treasurer, William Kealhofer, the board arranged to buy an automobile to serve as its next "book wagon." This autobuggy would have shelves like the ones in the original wagon, but its greater speed meant it could visit more customers in a shorter period of time. The Library hired a man to drive, and Ms. Chrissinger, who had worked with Ms. Titcomb for several years, was in charge of helping people with book selections. She was perfectly at home with the books available in the library, and now she set herself to learn about the people whose homes she would visit.

Rural customers had some specific tastes in books. There was less call for fiction than there was in the city, although some people did enjoy Western stories. There was much interest in informational books about growing crops, keeping accounts, carpentry, and even civil engineering. One woman borrowed many children's books and used them to teach her husband to read. Another woman, who lived in a very shabby, poor house where the windows were stuffed with rags, always looked for travel books about wonderfully exotic places very different from her own home. Ms. Chrissinger made sure to have those books in the bookmobile. During World War I she brought a copy of *Father of a Soldier* and other specially chosen titles to comfort the worried parents of a soldier fighting overseas. Still another customer argued with Ms. Chrissinger, insisting that novels were sinful and that only wicked people read them. Ms. Chrissinger brought her a copy of *Ben Hur* and urged her to read it. When the wagon returned, the woman was thrilled, announced it must be the best book ever written, and from then on she was grateful for "The Book Lady's" advice. Many other rural readers agreed, and Ms. Chrissinger often returned from her trips with gifts of flowers, fruit, and vegetables. Like Mary Titcomb and Joshua Thomas, she understood how important it was to have a personal connection with her customers.

The first true bookmobile flourished. Approximately 9,000 books were loaned out from it each year and it visited more than 700 families. Often each book that was borrowed was read by all members of the family and by their friends, as well. In 1916 the library bought a Koehler truck, which had seats for a chauffeur, as well as two passengers, and carried 500 books. Later trucks were built by the Dodge Company.

With her bookmobile solidly in place, Mary Titcomb turned her attention to professional training in library work. Her own training had happened entirely by chance, and she wanted young people who were interested in library work to have a solid, structured background. The apprenticeship program she designed included the study of literature, important points to consider in the choosing of books and materials for the library, and etiquette. The course of study was an early example of adult education, and it was very rare for such a small library to offer such comprehensive training. At that time, most library schools required a college degree for entrance. Ms. Titcomb's apprenticeship program was designed to give basic library training to girls who had a high school education. Once they mastered the skills she taught, they would be able to get work in a library and perhaps then be accepted at a library school. One of Mary Titcomb's pupils, Margaret Binklet Duvernet, followed that path. When she was a senior at the high school, she was allowed to take a course at the library. She loved books and quickly accepted the chance to study with Ms. Titcomb. She said Ms. Titcomb treated her students well and that they had the greatest respect for her. Upon her graduation, Margaret joined the library staff at a salary of $15 a month and worked both in the library itself and on the book wagon. She left Hagerstown to study at the Pratt Institute and upon graduation was hired to work at the Federal Reserve Library.

Mary Titcomb celebrated her 25th anniversary at the Washington County Free Library in 1926. Letters of congratulations came from every state and from some foreign countries as well. She was given a silver pitcher and a check for $750. She used the money to take a trip to Europe, and she created quite a stir when she went on an "aeroplane" from London to Paris. The idea that a woman of her age and station should not only travel to Europe all by herself and then do something as shocking as fly in an airplane set tongues wagging, reported the *Herald-Mail*. At the same time, the library raised funds to replace 1,000 worn books. One of the donors was a woman who lived in an isolated area of the county and who had used the book wagon years earlier. She pledged $1.50 of her chicken and egg money to support the library that had been so helpful to her.

Ms. Mary Titcomb, the painfully shy and fearful little girl, was remembered as a woman with initiative and vision and a devotion to her community and her library. Rather than a "frosty New Englander," she became known as a gracious and charming woman who loved the magic found in books and devoted her life to bringing that magic to everyone. Her bookmobile has been copied countless times. Mary died in 1932 after a brief illness and is buried in Sleepy Hollow Cemetery in Concord, Massachusetts, where she shares that final resting spot with Ralph Waldo Emerson, Nathaniel Hawthorne, and Henry David Thoreau.

Emily Hammond Wilson Walker, 1904-2007

Country Doctor

Emily Hammond Wilson Walker

Friends and family called her "Doc." At age thirteen, Emily Hammond knew that she wanted to be a doctor. It was not an easy path for a woman in the early part of the twentieth century and not one that her parents could easily afford. The Hammonds were not wealthy, but they were a well-established family in South Carolina. Her great grandfather, James Henry Hammond, had been Governor of the state from 1840 to 1842. Emily was born in 1904 at Redcliffe Plantation in Beech Island, South Carolina, which came into the family when her great grandfather married Catherine Redcliffe. Located on a cliff above the Savannah River and facing the Georgia shore, it was built in1859. It would be a favorite place for generations of Hammonds to gather for family celebrations. When Emily was six months old, her parents, Mary Gwynn and Christopher Hammond, moved to another family home, Kathwood, where they would raise their eight children. Because both of her parents came from large families, they had relatives along the eastern seaboard. Many of them would help Emily achieve her dream.

Emily remembered Kathwood as a wonderful place to grow up. It was a large piece of property that the family farmed. Black families who lived on the grounds helped with growing the crops and other chores to make Kathwood run smoothly. Family picnics, horseback riding, and swimming in a nearby creek provided the youngsters with a carefree childhood. Emily's aunt, Julia, often rode her horse from Redcliffe Plantation to visit them. Nothing was more exciting to Emily than to gallop back to Redcliffe during a thunderstorm wrapped in her Aunt Julia's cloak. The children walked a mile to attend school in a one-room building in Beech Island. A wood stove provided heat in the winter and the children sat on long benches by grade level. One teacher taught twenty students, grades one through seven. There were three students in Emily's class.

Christopher tried a number of ventures to provide for his growing family. Crops were the main source of income, but they were not always profitable. Prices set by out-of-state officials affected how much money farmers could get for a bale of cotton. Tomatoes might spoil on route to their destination because trains had no refrigerated cars. And a good growing season depended on good weather, which no one could control. To shore up family finances, Christopher found other ways to make money. He ground meal into flour for neighbors using a gristmill on the property. He also managed the town's general store and later he became a freight agent for the railroad at Kathwood Station, for which he was paid $15 a month. He made friends with train conductors who often brought him a barrel of oysters or some other treat for the family.

Eight children kept Mary Gwynn busy, as did the farm tenants. She helped with their births, illnesses, and deaths, often accompanied by Emily. Undoubtedly these outings greatly influenced the young girl in her decision to become a doctor. Mary Gwynn was the first Catholic in Beech Island and although this set her apart, everyone liked and admired her. She had been a teacher when she met Emily's father and was determined that her children be educated. When Emily announced that she wanted to be a doctor, her parents never discouraged her despite the financial hardship it would cause. Seeing how hard her parents worked was a good foundation for one of the earliest practicing female doctors in Maryland. She would draw upon their strengths as she confronted the challenges ahead.

Emily saw Baltimore for the first time when she went to Mt. Saint Agnes, a boarding school in the Mt. Washington area of the city. The family chose to send her north because there were no high schools near Beech Island. Two of Emily's aunts were alumnae of the school and they were able to obtain a scholarship for their niece. Emily was homesick and did not like the city. The following year, an uncle who was a priest helped her get a scholarship to St. Genevieve's in Asheville, North Carolina. Although she found the regimen strict, the school was closer to home. She graduated in a class of eight girls. "I was sixteen, and I was very ambitious,"[1] she said.

She hoped to go to Johns Hopkins Medical School. But first she had to take pre-med classes. Once again, Emily headed north to Baltimore to fulfill these requirements at Goucher College. She did not do well in German, and since it was a requirement for Hopkins, she had to rethink her plans.

Emily finished her pre-medical courses at the University of Georgia with the intent of entering the Medical College of Georgia at Augusta. Because she was not a Georgia state resident, another uncle, a judge in Augusta, sponsored her for admission to its medical school. Emily was accepted and each weekday she drove twelve miles to classes on unpaved roads in the family's small car.

Two other women joined Emily in the male dominated class at the college. One left during the first year and the second one the following year. Her fellow classmates said, "You know, we'd thought we'd lose you in the third year, and here you are still with us." Emily retorted, "Well I'm sorry to disappoint you, and I'd like to be accommodating; but I'm not going to quit."[2] They continued to tease her, especially in anatomy class. Each student was given a cadaver to study. If the teacher left the room they threw bits of human tissue about, hoping to make Emily faint. She did not. When the class had to observe an operation, Emily happily noted that many of her fellow male students became squeamish and had to leave the operating room. Emily watched the entire operation.

Emily worked hard and did well. Her brothers and sisters often heard, and if needed, corrected memorization assignments. One time she brought home human bones for an anatomy assignment. Horrified, her brothers and sisters were sure that the bones came with ghosts and were relieved when Emily took them back to the school. If she had time, she relaxed by gardening or horseback riding. In her third year of medical school, her parents gave her a horse. She named it "C2," after a carbon atom that had caused her difficulty in chemistry class. When she graduated from medical school in 1927, she was the only woman in the class and the second woman to graduate from the Medical College of Georgia.

After medical school and after passing state board examinations, doctors take further training through internships and residency programs in hospitals. When Emily applied for an internship at Willingford Hospital in Augusta, she was told that females were not wanted. The Central Georgia Railroad Hospital in Savannah did accept her for a residency position, but it was not without bias. She attended medical conferences but was excluded from social gatherings. The head of the hospital arranged meetings at a men's club and never changed the location so that Emily might be included. His wife, whom Emily had met several times earlier, now refused to speak to her. Doctors avoided her in the lunchroom and even the head nurse declined to invite her to join her table.

As all medical residents do, Emily worked very hard. She was constantly on call and only allowed one free weekend every month. The hospital invited her back for a second year, but did not increase her salary. Incensed, Emily said, "If you don't think I'm worth more now than when I came here, I can't stay."[3]

The young doctor returned to Kathwood and searched the employment section of the *Journal of the American Medical Association* for hospitals needing doctors. This was the height of the depression and Emily needed to find a job. Eventually a hospital in Portland, Maine, invited her to join its staff. She signed a contract and prepared to head north. Just before she left, she saw a notice for a research position at the Johns Hopkins Hospital. Since the train made a scheduled stop in Baltimore, Emily decided to look at the Hopkins job. She was able to get an interview, which went well, and she was told that she would hear in a few days. Emily explained that she had to know that afternoon, that she had a 4 P.M. train, and that she was expected to begin a job in Maine. When she called back at 3 P.M., she learned that the position was hers and that she was to begin the following day.

Emily enjoyed the research and liked meeting other members of the staff such as Thomas Turner, who would later become Dean of the Johns Hopkins Medical School, and Helen Taussig, the famous pediatric cardiologist. But she still did not like the city and often escaped to the country where her relatives, the Bowies, lived. At one of her aunt's dinner parties, a guest told Emily that Dr. Arthur Shipley, Chief of Surgery at the University of Maryland Hospital, was interviewing applicants to take over the medical practice of a doctor in southern Anne Arundel County who had recently died. Emily promptly contacted Dr. Shipley and during her interview, Emily told him about her medical background and how she had always wanted to be a country doctor. "You can go down there and make your own plans, but I want to tell you that you've got three strikes against you," he told her. "First, you're little and skinny; second, you're a woman, and nobody down there has ever seen a woman doctor; and third, you are a Catholic, which is anathema in that part of the world..."[4] Despite his reservations he sent her on her way with letters of recommendation.

Johns Hopkins gave Emily a leave of absence. She borrowed $1000 from an uncle and bought a desk, chairs, and a cot that would be her bed, as well as the examining table, a folding screen, and medications to begin her practice. She bought a car and made arrangements to rent a room from Mrs. Marion Hall. Mrs. Hall also offered the use of a summer kitchen in the back of the house for Emily's office. Two hurdles remained. She needed a Maryland driver's license and she needed a license to practice medicine in Maryland. South Carolina did not require driving licenses but Emily was able to pass the test with the help of a friendly employee at the Motor Vehicle Department. She took an oral exam for the state's medical license and passed that as well. Not realizing that she would often be paid with freshly cleaned chickens or fresh produce, she set up a fee schedule. An office visit would cost one dollar, home visits were two dollars, and home deliveries were fifteen dollars. She was "Doc" and she was ready to open her office.

Mrs. Hall introduced her to residents of South County, another name for southern Anne Arundel County, but patients were slow to accept the new lady doctor. After a few weeks her first patient arrived—a dog. When people realized that Emily had successfully stitched the animal's injury, she began getting patients. It took time to get people to come to her office for treatment. They preferred that she come to them. Emily did not rule out house calls, but since she was almost the only doctor in the area, office visits were more efficient. She ignored the area's segregation policies. Everyone sat in one waiting room and was seen on a first come, first served basis.

Practicing medicine in a rural area in the early part of the twentieth century was difficult. Bad roads, bad weather, delivering babies, and fighting illnesses before antibiotics were discovered were challenges for Emily. In southern Maryland there were only two paved roads, Route 2 and Route 408. Remaining roads were dirt and were almost impassable during certain months. If patients could not get to her, Emily drove as far as she could and then walked the remaining distance carrying her medical bag. Or she rode a horse. Women did not receive prenatal care at that time. Consequently, Emily never knew the health status of the expectant mother until she arrived to deliver the baby. Because sedatives had not been discovered, it was necessary for women to breath from chloroform soaked pads to relieve pain during the delivery. Emily met all the challenges with persistence, grace, and when needed, a sense of humor. As she told Dr. Shipley when he expressed his concerns about her success as a country doctor, she was tough.

To Emily's surprise she also became the area's dentist. White dentists refused to see black patients even in emergency cases. Many blacks had severe dental problems and Emily often treated those with abscessed teeth.

As more people gained confidence in her, her practice grew. Next, she needed to have admitting privileges at the Annapolis hospital, but the hospital doctors opposed having a woman join them. When she finally received staff privileges, the hospital's nurses made it difficult for Emily by slowing down the admitting process for her patients. However, in time she earned the respect of both doctors and nurses.

Sometimes reaching patients could take hours or days. One rainy night, a neighbor who had been reluctant to accept the new doctor called Emily in the middle of the night in great pain. She tried to drive to his home but got stuck in the mud. She called the patient and said that someone would have to come and get her. A farmhand tried but his truck also got stuck in the mud. Finally, he returned in a tractor and took Emily to his sick employer. Emily was sure that the man had appendicitis but there was no way to get him to the hospital that night. She gave him a shot of morphine to relieve his pain hoping that his appendix would not burst. The next morning Emily borrowed a horse and buggy and took her patient to the paved road where he was then taken to the hospital by car. Doctors immediately removed his appendix. Afterwards, the neighbor had nothing but praise for the lady doctor.

Many people developed pneumonia in the winter because houses did not have central heating and few had indoor plumbing. Without the antibiotics that are available today, there was little Emily could do for those who became sick and many people died. Emily was the first doctor in the area to use an oxygen tent to treat pneumonia patients. She was also the first person in the area to diagnose Rocky Mountain spotted fever when she was called to see a feverish child who had been bitten by a tick. When the child developed a rash that was symptomatic of the disease, it confirmed Emily's diagnosis. It was the first case in southern Maryland and doctors from Johns Hopkins came to observe the child, who fortunately survived.

Phone lines were party lines in those days, which meant that more than one person used the same phone line. This too, was a problem for the new doctor. People on Emily's phone line could listen to her conversations, making patient confidentiality impossible. Nor was it unusual for people to interrupt Emily and offer their own remedies to the caller. Another person disliked the phone's beeping noise and took it off the hook. When that happened no one on that party line could receive phone calls. Emily asked the phone company to intervene.

The young doctor was too busy establishing a medical practice to have much time for a social life. There were occasional bridge games and dances, but there was no romance until she met John Wilson. They became engaged but it was a rocky beginning because of their religious differences. Emily's Uncle Keen, a Catholic priest, wanted the groom, who was Episcopalian, to agree to raise their children in the Catholic Church. When John's close friend refused to be his best man, it was the first time that Emily personally experienced prejudice against Catholicism. As a result, they postponed the wedding. John's mother wrote Emily saying that she hoped that they could work things out. Caring deeply for each other, they did. Although neither converted to the other's religion, Emily agreed to let their future children make their own decisions about religion when they turned thirteen. They were married at Redcliffe in 1932.

The couple lived with John's mother on the Wilson family estate, Old Town. Crops and animals were raised on its 600 acres, which had been in John's family for generations. Emily set up an office in the back of the house, but when patients began to appear at Old Town unannounced and at any hour, Emily bought a building, called the Tea House, on Route 2 for her office. The Wilsons' two sons, John and Christopher, were born while the family lived at Old Town.

By now Doc had 2000 patients. Her sons remember making house calls with their mother, often falling asleep in the car waiting for her. John remembered that he had not had chickenpox and because it was less dangerous for the young, his mother took him to visit a child who had the disease so John would be exposed. She preferred treating patients in her office because they could receive better care, but it remained a difficult battle. Because there were no blood tests or diagnostic machines then, Emily relied on her skills of observation as the best way to treat patients. She found that many times family members of different generations were susceptible to the same ailments. This was particularly true with ulcers and respiratory illnesses.

In 1947 the Wilsons bought Obligation Farm, whose main house had been built in 1671. Emily knew the house had potential, but years of vacancy were readily apparent. Wanderers had stripped tobacco in the den and housed pigs in many of the rooms. Fumes from a remaining distillery on the top floor permeated the entire house. Plumbing, heat, electricity, and water were nonexistent. It took five years to restore the house.

During this time the Wilsons hired tenant farmers to take care of the tobacco fields. They were an unreliable group and often quit. This happened one January when there was a barn full of tobacco leaves waiting to be stripped for the spring market. Emily needed to sell the crop in order to recover her expenses and she was grateful when some of her patients came to the rescue and stripped the tobacco. Emily piled the crop onto a tractor and drove it to the market, but the experience reminded her of her father's difficulties with his cotton crops and she was relieved when they no longer grew tobacco.

A year after moving into their new house, John Wilson died of a heart attack. Maintaining Obligation Farm drained the family finances. Although John had worked at the comptroller's office in Annapolis, in those days the state of Maryland did not provide a pension plan. Emily obtained scholarships to the Hill School in Pennsylvania for the boys and they spent summers at Kathwood, which they loved. This allowed Emily time to oversee the farm and to treat her patients.

Emily worked hard to expand medical care for citizens of South County. She served as Assistant County Examiner and was active in the County Medical Society. She stressed the need for a prenatal clinic and when it opened, it was a tremendous resource for expectant mothers. In 1951 Emily was made Chief of Staff of the Annapolis hospital, twenty-two years after she was almost refused privileges. During this time she oversaw the enlargement of the hospital and the creation of a system of department heads. When The American Medical Association wanted doctors to divide themselves into specialties, physicians in Annapolis resented having doctors from Johns Hopkins become heads of surgery, medicine, and other new specialties, but Emily provided guidance and reassurance during this difficult time.

As the years progressed, Emily's practice became quite large. She had been elected twice to be Chief of Staff at the Annapolis hospital. There just was not enough time to give her patients adequate care, make house calls, hospital rounds, and manage the farm. She needed help, but what could she do? She decided to eliminate home deliveries. Patients could go to the hospital in Annapolis and clinics had been built nearby that provided care for African Americans. Doctor friends and senior medical students agreed to relieve her on Saturdays.

Although Emily remained a widow for thirty years, she had an active social life. She was lively, fun, and neighbors loved it when she accepted their invitations. It was not until she gave an engagement party for a niece in Beech Island in 1972 that she reconnected with her high school beau, Albert Tupper Walker, who had recently lost his wife. After they married, Tup moved north and adapted to Emily's schedule and to country life. When Emily retired in 1982, her patients had a hard time accepting it but Tup was delighted. They traveled extensively and spent fourteen happy years together before Tup died in 1988.

Emily kept her spunk and sense of adventure well into her later years. When she was 91, family members in Florida invited her to spend Thanksgiving with them. She bought a new car to make the trip. When the saleswoman looked at her driver's license, she thought there was a mistake. The license said she was born in 1904. Emily told her that her eyesight was just fine, the license was correct.

Emily Hammond Wilson Walker died in July 2007 at the age of 103. People remembered her as a pioneer in medicine and race relations. Over the years, she earned the respect of her peers in the way she dealt with the existing gender bias in medicine. People respected and loved her because of her immeasurable persistence, courage, and kindness. Whenever obstacles occurred, she found more than one way to solve problems. She adapted to whatever the occasion called for, whether exhibiting bravery among a classroom of male medical students or convincing a rural population to accept her as their doctor. She dealt gracefully with changes in the medical world and welcomed new advancements in medical care. Generations of families in South County praised their lady doctor.

Verda Welcome, 1907 – 1990
Educator and Legislator

In 1959, when Verda Welcome took the oath of office as a delegate to Maryland's General Assembly representing Baltimore City's fourth district, she became the first of two African American women to do so. Although she was not a seasoned politician, she had worked with many interracial groups. She had thought long and hard before running for a seat in Maryland's House of Delegates, but she knew that the only way to eliminate segregation was to have someone represent African Americans in a place where policy decisions were made.

Women, and certainly African American women, were unlikely to

Verda Welcome

be voted into positions of power. But in many ways Verda Welcome was at the right place at the right time, as her entry into politics coincided with the beginning of the Civil Rights movement. She introduced several bills, most of which took years to become laws. This did not disturb her because she realized that it would take a long time for change to occur. Legislators learned to respect Verda's quiet determination. In time her foresight and negotiating abilities helped propel Maryland's Civil Rights movement forward.

Verda was born in 1907, the third of sixteen children born to John and Ella Freeman. Having a heritage of being free blacks who owned land, the Freemans were proud people, a trait they passed on to their children. The family lived in Uree, now known as Lake Lure, a town in the far northwest corner of North Carolina's Blue Ridge Mountains, where John supported his family by farming. Verda remembered her childhood as one filled with plenty of love, plenty of food, and plenty of hard work. She also remembered that her parents stressed the importance of self-respect. In the future she would draw on this and other strengths inherited from her parents to overcome prejudice against her race, gender, and political aspirations.

Verda attended the Mary B. Mullen Institute, a nearby integrated church school. It was Verda's first experience with white people and she learned that there was a far larger world than her corner of North Carolina. Hoping that Verda would become a teacher, Ella sent her to the Peabody Institute in Troy, North Carolina, to take education courses. After finishing what would be the equivalent of a junior high school education, Verda taught elementary school for a year in Greenville. It was not easy. Her students had different levels of ability and many were taller than she. Verda knew she could be a good teacher with more training, but she was pleased that her students responded to her kindness and supportive attitude.

When Ella died in childbirth in 1927, Verda was overcome with grief. She adored her mother. Her father wanted the older children, including Verda, to remain at home and care for their younger siblings. Verda knew that her mother's primary concern was furthering her children's education and that Ella would not approve of her John's decision.

At her mother's funeral, a friend told Verda about his educational experience at a Northern school. The thought appealed to the young girl and she contacted distant relatives in Wilmington, Delaware. In exchange for room and board, Verda did light housekeeping chores and was able to finish her high school education. Her relatives suggested that she go to Coppin Normal School, now Coppin State College, for a two-year teacher-training program. Upon arriving in Baltimore, she again lived with distant relatives but she needed money to support herself and to pay the tuition. The Great Depression made this almost impossible, as jobs were hard to find. At a church function she met an older woman, Anne Harris, who helped the young girl find a summer job in Ocean City, Maryland. Anne had worked at the resort's Majestic Hotel and persuaded the manager to hire Verda. This was the first time that she had been employed by white people. She was polite and did her job, washing and drying the hotel guests' bathing suits, but she never forgot the racial injustices that she saw that summer.

Using the money she earned in Ocean City, Verda enrolled at Coppin. She returned to the same job the following summer so that she could afford to finish her teacher-training program, which she did in 1932. Knowing how demoralized young blacks felt at that time, Anne Harris began forum sessions on Sunday nights where they could discuss their concerns. Verda met her future husband, Henry Welcome, at one of the Sunday discussions. The medical student from Honduras, who was committed to being the best and doing his best, impressed her. When he first proposed, Verda said no. She was content with having him as a pal and called him, "Palie." But Henry was persistent and slowly Verda fell in love with the serious medical student. They waited until Henry's last year in medical school, and were married in December 1935. He remained "Palie" throughout their married life.

In 1936 Palie obtained an internship at Provident Hospital. Verda taught in Baltimore City while working on her bachelor's degree at Morgan College, now Morgan State University. Although she could not change the fact that Baltimore's segregated school system led to inferior schools and instruction for black students, she knew that having a master's degree in education would improve her teaching. But Maryland's institutions of higher learning did not accept African American students. Instead, they went to out-of-state schools to receive advanced degrees. Verda spent the next few summers taking courses at New York State University, from which she received her master's degree in education in 1943.

The Welcomes bought a house in Baltimore's Fourth District and settled into their routines, Verda teaching and Palie working at Provident Hospital. Family members and many young people often stayed with them. One young girl, Mary Sue, became the Welcome's adopted daughter. Verda began to join organizations that were fighting prejudice and racism. She was the regional director of the National Council of Negro Women and when Palie was admitted to the American College of Surgeons, they became active in the National Medical Association, an organization for African American doctors. They were grateful for the life they led, but Verda was ready for something more.

In 1945 she left teaching to become an activist. Jobs were plentiful because of the city's port, but Baltimore's expanding population after World War II presented problems, especially in areas where black families lived. Zoning laws were inadequate. Streets were crowded and owners of large buildings converted them into apartments containing too many people. There were no organizations to help newcomers to the city and citizens were frustrated by the lack of concern shown by city officials. Believing in her father's value of giving back to society, Verda became involved in different community organizations, among them, the Northwest Improvement Association.

Baltimore citizens first took note of Verda Welcome when she organized a group to fight fire escapes. The law required apartment owners to have adequate numbers of them based on the number of occupants in the building. As landlords crammed people into buildings to get more revenue, they built fire escapes in front of houses, as well as in the back, without posting a notice. People objected to these eyesores. When it came to Verda's attention that the law said that a permit had to be posted ten days prior to erecting a fire escape, she and others met with the mayor and zoning board. Their complaints resulted in the city passing an ordinance that prohibited fire escapes on the fronts of buildings on main streets. Feeling empowered by this success, they began to fight for improvement in other municipal services. They hired Juanita Jackson Mitchell, a prominent civil rights activist, to be their lawyer.

As Verda became more involved in committee work, she realized that the post war boom had created a group of economically successful African Americans who were beginning to challenge segregation. They had fought in a war for freedom but at home, nothing had changed. They disliked the restrictions on home ownership locations and they resented not being served in restaurants or having the freedom to try on clothes in department stores owned by white people.

What would be the impetus for change? Quite simply, more African Americans needed to vote. Baltimore City was divided into districts that elected delegates and state senators to represent them in the state legislature. The number of delegates was based on the number of people who lived in the district. In the 1950s two factions influenced votes. Political bosses controlled districts and their endorsement of candidates guaranteed victory at the polls. Secondly, African Americans historically belonged to the Republican Party, which meant that their votes had little influence in Maryland, a Democratic state. The only hope for change was to get African Americans to elect someone to represent them in Annapolis. There was much to do to educate her people about the voting process.

Verda joined Victorine Adams and her organization, the Colored Women's Democratic Club, when she noticed how effective its members were in educating people about the importance of voting. Verda and other women gave informative seminars at community centers and various organizations. They registered new voters and encouraged people to vote in future elections. They gave these workshops during election years as well as off years, thereby insuring a large base of voters.

In 1957 Mayor Thomas D'Alesandro wanted to build a civic center in Druid Hill Park, located in the fourth district. Families opposed building in an area that provided wide- open places for their children to play. Verda developed a broad base of supporters to oppose the Mayor, but he was a powerful force and the City Council voted in favor of the proposed location. Verda, with the help of the lawyer Hyman Pressman, filed a suit against the plan. The Judge ruled against the city and Verda was ecstatic. Throughout these years she had become fascinated with the inner workings of the political process. She found it exciting and she was ready to enter the political arena.

After long talks with Palie, she decided to enter the race for a seat in the House of Delegates in 1958. At the time, African Americans and a large Jewish community were the predominant groups living in the fourth district. Jack Pollock, a savvy political boss, heavily influenced the latter group. Verda knew that he would not support her and she joined an all-black coalition of both Democrats and Republicans. Determined to win, Verda opened an office on North Avenue and drove her welcome wagon throughout the district. She ran a grass roots campaign and knocked on everyone's door, blacks and whites, to solicit support. There was much political maneuvering before the election, but Verda won as an independent Democrat. More importantly, her election proved that it was possible to win without Jack Pollock's backing.

In 1959 the fourth district's representatives, Verda Welcome, Irma Dixon, and J. Alvin Jones went to Annapolis eager to make changes for Maryland's African Americans. But recognizing that many delegates resisted integration, Verda introduced civil rights legislation slowly. She developed lobbying techniques and formed coalitions among white senators for their support. Her constituents wanted faster action, but Verda assured them that by creating alliances, she would win. She presented several bills during her first session and some almost passed. She would need to work harder in the next session if changes were to occur.

Support for a public accommodations bill was accelerated when Verda experienced racial discrimination personally at a state legislature convention in Ocean City during the summer of 1960. When she and a colleague went to the hotel desk to register, the manager refused to rent them a room. Instead he offered them servants' rooms in the basement. Despite protests from their white colleagues, the hotel manager would not change his mind. Verda was irate and returned to Annapolis ready to propose a bill that would allow anyone to sleep, eat, or use the bathroom in any public facility. Verda spent hours building support for the bill, but it was defeated. It would not be a law for several more years.

An undercurrent of racial unrest was growing in America in the 1960s. Blacks and whites organized demonstrations protesting existing segregation policies. People supported Martin Luther King and wanted equality for everyone. Demonstration marches in the South became violent and as the horrific events of the 1960s unfolded, Verda traveled to the Deep South to witness the protests herself. What she saw reinforced her commitment to continue working for civil rights legislation.

In 1962 Verda decided to run for state senator. If she won, she, not Jack Pollock, would be in control of the fourth district, which would give her more influence in Annapolis. She won the election, making her the first African American woman to be elected to a state senate. Some people openly criticized her because of her sex. Only men could stand up to a governor, they said. Ignoring her critics she pushed for civil rights and did stand up to governors. Years later Verda reflected, "All my life, I never felt inferior to men. I insisted on doing whatever my brother did. Mother would say, 'you can't do that, you're a girl.' That angered me."[1]

By 1963 people recognized Verda as a prominent civil rights leader. She had been instrumental in the reapportionment of state districts that allowed more blacks to be elected to the state legislature. She had worked on the ever-expanding public accommodations bill and, with the help of Governor Tawes, succeeded in getting a version of the bill passed. While many people admired her, many became enemies. Returning home in April 1964, she was wounded when three people fired guns at her car. Fortunately, she was not seriously injured. Although she and Palie were concerned about her safety, Verda refused to back down. "I just couldn't run away…I represented something to a lot of people and I couldn't let them down…"[2] The gunmen were caught and put in jail. Verda and others felt that there were political reasons behind the shooting and she remained watchful.

By the end of her first session as state senator, the legislature had passed a law requiring equal pay for men and women who performed the same job. Maryland had a standing law that prohibited intermarriage between blacks and whites. Feeling strongly that marriage should not be regulated, Verda worked to repeal the law. That would not happen until later, nor would open housing, but she had planted the seeds for change. The state's population had shifted, leaving many areas without representation in Annapolis. A newly formed reapportionment committee would change this. At the same time, Verda wanted to change city district boundaries so that there would be more districts whose resident majority was African American. If this happened, the district's vote would increase the number of black representatives in the state legislature.

Changes did happen. Throughout the 1970s Verda helped pass laws to regulate the automobile industry and secured money to improve Provident Hospital, an important facility for the city's African Americans. When businessmen wanted to build a fast food restaurant outside Mondawin Mall, Verda opposed it. The Motor Vehicle Department had just moved to the Mall, thereby increasing neighborhood traffic. Additional traffic would be detrimental for nearby residents. Although Verda knew that she could not change people's smoking habits, she proposed legislation that forced restaurants to have both smoking and nonsmoking areas for its patrons. She helped regulate gun control laws and made it legal for citizens to register to vote by mail. She pushed for Morgan State to become a University and she created a commission on African American History and Culture.

Verda Welcome worked hard to improve civil rights in Maryland. It was not always easy. Political machines and bosses dictated votes and alliances constantly changed. Verda had the ability to create coalitions and to make people work together and she learned how to work with governors whether they were sympathetic to the Civil Rights movement or not. People respected her sincerity and commitment. She remained above reproach, never yielding to bribes. She displayed unquestionable courage in her fight against segregation during her twenty-year career as a state senator. In 1988 she was elected to the Maryland Women's Hall of Fame. Verda Welcome died in 1990.

Deborah Yow, 1942–
College Athletic Director

People in Gibsonville, North Carolina, knew that all four Yow children were athletic. Ron, the only boy, won a football scholarship to Clemson and his older sister Kay played and then coached college basketball. The youngest in the family, Susan, was considered the best player in the family. And then there was Debbie, who described herself as the classic middle girl. It was clear she loved a challenge and that she could excel.

Debbie's mother owned a beauty shop next to their house and when she was busy with customers it was Debbie's job to start dinner. Conversation around the table centered on sports— who had a game, and where and when the game would be played. All the children participated actively in sports. Athletics were part of the entire family's fabric. Before she was married, Debbie's

Debbie Yow

mother worked and played on a company basketball team in North Carolina. Her daughters followed her example.

Debbie did well in elementary school and she developed a love of reading. She shone in English classes in her elementary and high school years and each success she had encouraged her to work harder. However, she was less fascinated by math, which she found difficult and unrewarding. She settled into the habit of not applying herself in that class. The school system had some excellent interscholastic athletic programs for girls, and she continued to play basketball through high school and looked forward to continuing to play in college. Debbie made some poor choices during her first years at college, however, and flunked out by the end of her second year. The bright young woman who could excel was floundering.

She spent more than a year working at fast-food restaurants and then gathered herself together. She had dreamed of going to college and playing basketball there. With a clearer sense of purpose, she followed her sister Kay to Elon College. Debbie still loved basketball and at Elon she played for a coach she knew and respected—Kay. She decided to major in English because she knew she had talent and because, as in high school, her professors encouraged her.

After graduating from Elon, she taught English and coached at the high school, then the collegiate level. A no-nonsense teacher, she emphasized grammar and mechanics, required her students to diagram sentences, and assigned thought-provoking books like Pearl S. Buck's *The Good Earth* and George Orwell's *Animal Farm*. Her classes, which included some challenging students, were run on the "my way or the highway" principle.[1] It was clear who was in charge. She was active on the basketball court as well, and from 1976 to 1985 she coached basketball at the University of Kentucky, Oral Roberts University, and the University of Florida. Then she began to move toward administrative work.

From 1985 to 1987, while she studied for a master's degree in counseling, Debbie worked as the assistant athletic director of the Florida Gators. At the end of her time in Florida she was hired as the associate athletic director at the University of North Carolina at Greensboro, where she served from 1987 to 1990. Now, with several years experience, she was ready to make a major move. In 1990 Debbie Yow was named athletic director at Saint Louis University.

A university athletic director was usually a senior administrator, responsible for all aspects of all the school's sports programs. Traditionally, a man held that job and it was often given to a successful senior coach who was ready to leave active work on the playing field to younger men. In contrast, Debbie was young, she was not moving up from a coaching position at the school, and, of course, she was not a man. Her husband, Bill Bowden, cautioned her that the job would have many difficult challenges. He was right, it would, and she would meet them directly.

Some people at Saint Louis University felt that her vision for the athletic program was too broad, too unrealistic, and clearly unreachable. She was not convinced. An earnest local sportswriter sat down with her and explained why she could not be successful in that job. She listened politely but continued to follow her own path. Further, the men's basketball coach, who had worked hard to improve his team's performance and was popular within the community, announced publicly that he did not think she was a good choice for the job. She answered with action. Within two years, she succeeded in hiring a successful and high-profile basketball coach. He led the team to the NCAA tournament for the first time in 37 years and attendance at games doubled.

Her energy and vision made a difference to the program. Under her leadership the school joined the new Great Midwest Conference, she was able to hire several well-known coaches, and she pushed for the formation of a club to encourage private donations to the athletic department. By 1990 that club would have more than a thousand members. She focused on the students, and with her guidance the number of athletic scholarships was raised and the graduation rate rose to 92%. It was not always a smooth and comfortable path. Early in her tenure she wanted to improve the ticket sale process. It was not successful and left many alumni infuriated. Characteristically, she learned from her mistake and did not repeat it. By the time she left, most of her earlier detractors had become admirers.

In 1994 Debbie Yow was hired as the athletic director at the University of Maryland College Park. As a Division I school, nationally known for its sports, its opportunities for athletes and athletic administrators were attractive and exciting. As she had at Saint Louis, she immediately ran into opposition because she was a woman. There was open criticism from some boosters of the athletic program who expressed disappointment and anger that the job would not go to a man. "They hired a skirt!" one irritated booster complained. She had faced that reaction before and she was able to handle it with poise and self-confidence. "Leadership is not a gender issue,"[4] she said.

The first major challenge that she faced at Maryland would be difficult to fix. The athletic department was deeply in debt and had not had a balanced budget for ten years.

The debt was over fifty million dollars, and it was clear to her that it had been ignored by earlier administrations. She felt an atmosphere of carelessness extended to other aspects of the athletic program as well, with budgets, time sheets, and other details sometimes being handled in a slipshod way. She went to work immediately to improve the department's finances. Her strategy included trimming costs where appropriate. She announced a cutback in janitorial expenses, even, for a time, vacuuming her own office. During her first thirteen years, the department paid off its $8 million dollar operating debt and cut its facility debt from $43 million to $8 million. She pushed to put major emphasis on marketing and to develop creative fund-raising ideas. During those years overall fund-raising for the athletic department rose from just over $2 million to just under $25 million dollars. The department benefited when the board of regents agreed to allow some talented out-of-state athletes to pay in-state tuition rates. Corporate sponsorships more than doubled after she arrived at College Park.

She worked to make sure that the program operated in a financially responsible way, and she spent money to support her vision. Developing a reputation as a builder of programs, she oversaw the creation of new fields and added updated and new facilities to support the athletic teams. The Comcast Center, built in 2002, housed the administrative offices; a basketball facility that holds more than 17,000 people; and a gym for volleyball, gymnastics, and wrestling with room for 1500 spectators. In addition, it had a multipurpose room used for meetings, press conferences, and banquets, and a large academic support center for the student-athletes.

A goal-oriented, competitive person, Debbie appreciated the university teams' progress and celebrated the successes they earned on the field. At the same time she also urged the more than 700 student athletes to work hard in their studies and succeed in the classroom. The dream of playing professional sports can end with just one injury, she pointed out. It is not an accident that the academic support center was located in the Comcast Center, side by side with the athletic department's administrative offices. With few exceptions, graduation rates in all sports increased and the athletes' overall graduation rate rose to the highest point in the school's history. Maryland became one of the nation's leaders in its athletes' academic success. Over the years, Debbie herself exemplified academic success, completing both her master's and doctoral degrees while she continued to work.

New leadership often means new people, and there were changes in personnel during her first years at Maryland. Some changes were unremarkable, while others, like firing football coach Mark Duffner in 1995, caused an uproar. She was frank and forthright when she talked with the press about the reasons she fired Duffner, and her comments angered some prominent supporters of the football program but she did not back down. Noting there are different styles of leadership, she described herself as "type A, 1-2-3" rather than a warm and fuzzy person.[2] She stressed that teamwork, one of her major goals, was an art form. Over the years other members of the department left Maryland to take jobs with more responsibility, and she pointed out that good people would always have the opportunity to move on to other jobs.

The University of Maryland prospered and so did Debbie. Her efforts were recognized across the country. She was elected president of the National Association of Collegiate Directors of Athletics in 2001, was chosen as one of the twenty most influential people in intercollegiate athletics by *Sports Business Journal*, and won the Maddox Sport Management Award given by the United States Sports Academy for excellence in athletic administration. She was chosen to serve as one of the fifteen commissioners on the US Department of Education's Commission on Opportunities in Athletics, reviewing the progress of the antidiscrimination law in college athletics.

The author of numerous books and articles, she was listed as both an author and an editor of *Strategic Planning for College Athletics*, and with her husband, Bill Bowden, and others, she wrote *Stress in College Athletics: Causes, Consequences, Coping*. She teamed with James Humphrey to write *Adult Guide to Children's Team Sports* in 2002, and addressed the issues of competition and stress. She emphasized that a child's self-worth should not be tied to his or her athletic ability. Further, she acknowledged that competition could be negative and cause stress, but she said many good things, including improved physical fitness, came from athletic competition when properly managed by adults. Also, she pointed out that the world is competitive and competing helps teach young people coping skills. As an athlete learns to compete, he or she should be aware of the mind as well as the body. Both athletes and those who work with them should be alert for signs of stress and should develop strategies to deal with it, she said.

She took a special interest in women who were interested in becoming athletic directors. As a leader in this nontraditional role for women, she took exceptional care to tell prospective AD's about her job. It was a difficult balance: she wanted to be honest and straightforward, yet she did not want to be so discouraging that they would not try. The job itself presented a range of challenges. It also required Debbie to be out of her comfort zone much of the time. To relax and have fun, she and Bill visited their families or simply went to a good movie or to a restaurant. Her faith, which began to develop when she was in her early twenties, helped her, and her family's closeness was a constant support.

She advised young people to learn to think and to refuse to be satisfied with things as they are. "You can do better than just make it,"[3] she said. Tradition deserved respect, she noted, but innovation would lead the future. She valued people who came to work on time and also worked hard, and she felt there could be no substitute for surrounding yourself with the right people. When asked what she took the most pride in, she answered persistence and perseverance—that she fought through the tough times and did not quit. The classic middle child, who so disliked math and who failed in her first attempt at college, became a skilled and confident leader who took charge of hundreds of student athletes and an annual budget of millions of dollars. Debbie Yow chose a career in a field she loved, followed a nontraditional path within it, and pursued her goals with energy and enthusiasm.

After sixteen successful years at Maryland, Debbie was asked to be the athletic director at North Carolina State University. She accepted the offer, signed a five-year contract, and returned to her native state.

Bibliography

Florence Riefle Bahr

"Bahr Family Collection 1928-2001," (The Maryland Historical Society).

Bahr, Leonard. Personal Interview, August 20, 2007.

Bahr, Mary S. Personal Interviews, August 6, 2007 and August 24, 2007.

Ballenger, Connie. "History in a Doll's House," *The Howard County Times*, January 28, 1988.

Breen, Robert G. "A Versatile Artist," *The Baltimore Sun*, October 16, 1964.

Dawson, Jack. "A Family of Artists," *The Sun Magazine*, January 10, 1982.

Dorsey, John. "Art by Bahr," *The Baltimore Sun*, January 2, 1997.

"Florence Bahr's Passion Fire Victim: Works of Prolific Elkridge Artist Endures in Sketches and Paintings," *The Baltimore Sun*, January 15, 1998.

Fox, Elizabeth B. Online Interview, August 20, 2007.

Fox, Maurice. Online Interview, August 20, 2007.

"Florence Riefle Bahr's Show," *Gardens, Houses, and People*, February 1950.

"Florence Riefle Bahr," Maryland Art Source. (www.marylandartsource.org/artists/detail_000000131.html).

"Florence Riefle Bahr," Maryland Women's Hall of Fame. (Maryland State Archives, www.msa.md.gov/msa/educ/exhibits/womenshall/html/bahr.html).

"Painter In Musical Family Would Rather Draw Than Eat," *The Baltimore Sun*, June 29, 1936.

Stegman, Carolyn. *Women of Achievement in Maryland History*. (Forest Park, MD: Anaconda Press, 2002, 281-282).

Chapter Notes

1. Interview with Len Bahr. August 20, 2007.
2. Ibid
3. Ibid
4. Interview with Mary Bahr. August 6, 2007.
5. Interview with Len Bahr. August 20, 2007.

Helen Delich Bentley

Cohn, Meridith. "Port 'Godmother' Honored: Maryland Salutes Helen Delich Bentley, Longtime Champion of Baltimore's Maritime Industry," *The Baltimore Sun*, June 2, 2006.

Bentley, Helen Delich. Personal Interview, April 2007.

Helen Delich Bentley. "A Few Good Women: Advancing the Cause for Women in the U.S. Government," Oral History Transcript. (Pennsylvania State University, Special Collections, www.afgw.libraries.psu.edu/profiles/bentley.html).

Helen Delich Bentley Collection. (The University of Baltimore Langsdale Special Collections. Box 1).

"TV Show Wins Atlas Award: Miss Helen Delich," *Marine News*, 1957.

Warlow, Mary. "Helen Delich Bentley," *Smart Woman*, July/August 2006, 10-11.

Chapter Notes

1. Interview with Helen Delich Bentley, April 2007.

2. Ibid
3. Ibid

Margaret Brent

Adams, Anne. "Margaret Brent, First Woman to Request the Vote," *History's Women Newsletter*. (www.historyswomen.com/1stWomen/MargaretBrent.htm).

Baker, Ann. "Margaret Brent (ca. 1601-ca. 1671)," *Maryland History Leaflet No. 1*. (Maryland State Archives).

Carr, Lois Green. "Margaret Brent—A Brief History," Notes on Margaret Brent, copyright Dr. Lois Green Carr.(Historic St. Mary's City Commission, 2002).

Henretta, James. "Margaret Brent: A Woman of Property," *The Early America Review*. (www.earlyamerica.com/review/1998/brent.html).

James, Edward T., ed. *Notable American Women: A Biographical Dictionary*. (Cambridge, MA: Harvard University Press, 1971).

Masson, Margaret W. "Margaret Brent. c1601-c1671: Lawyer, Landholder—Entrepreneur," *Notable Maryland Women,* Ed. Winifred G. Helmes. (Cambridge, MD: Tidewater Publishers, 1977).

Spruill, Julia Cherry. "Mistress Margaret Brent, Spinster," *Maryland Historical Magazine*, 29, December 1934, 259-269.

Anna Ella Carroll

Coryell, Janet L. *Neither Heroine Nor Fool: Anna Ella Carroll of Maryland*. (Kent, OH: Kent State University Press, 1990).

Couzins, Phoebe W. *The Military Genius of the War, Anna Ella Carroll Author of the Tennessee Campaign*. (St. Lois: 1882).

Greenbie, Sydney, and Marjorie Barstow Greenbie. *Anna Ella Carroll and Abraham Lincoln*. (Manchester, Maine: University of Tampa Press, in cooperation with Falmouth Publishing House: 1952).

Larson, C. K. *Great Necessities: The Life, Times and Writings of Anna Ella Carroll*. (Philadelphia: Random House, 2004).

Noble, Hollister. *Woman with a Sword: The Biographical Novel of Anna Ella Carroll of Maryland*. (New York: Doubleday, 1948).

Eugenie Clark

Churchman, Deborah. "It's Shark-Fin Rides—Not Soup—For This Ichthyologist," *The Christian Science Monitor,* January 4, 1982.

Clark, Eugenie. *Lady With a Spear*. (New York: Harper & Brothers, 1953).

Cozzi, Dr. J. "Coz." "The Lady, The Sharks, and the Lab They Founded," *Mote Magazine* (Mote Marine Laboratory, 2005, www.mote.org)

Dr. Eugenie Clark Homepage. (www.sharklady.com)

"Eugenie Clark (1922 – present)," Explorers Archive. (Wings WorldQuest, Inc., http://explore.wingsworldquest.org/eugenie_clark).

"Eugenie Clark—The Shark Lady." *Dive Global*. (www.diveglobal.com/photography_film/the_greats/clarke.asp).

"Eugenie Clark, Ph.D." Maryland's Women Hall of Fame (Maryland State Archives, www.msa.md.gov/msa/educ/exhibits/womenshall/html/clark.html).

Krueger, Curtis. "At 83, She's Still Diving for Research," *St. Petersburg Times Online*, March 19, 2006. (www.sptimes.com/2006/03/19/State/At_83__she_s_still_di.shtml).

Krueger, Curtis. "Curiosity Drove Her to Become 'Shark Lady,'" *St. Petersburg Times Online*, March 18, 2006. (www.sptimes.com/2006/03/18/Tampabay/Curiosity_drove_her_t.shtml).

Lee, Carol E. "Mote Founder's Fascination with Fish Still Strong," *Herald Tribune.com* (www.heraldtribune.com/apps/pbcs.dll/article?AID=2007705040838).

Polking, Kirk. *Oceanographers and Explorers of the Sea*. (Springfield, NJ: Enslow Publishers, 1999, 63-72).

Prescott, Orville. "Books of the Times," *The New York Times,* July 17, 1953.

"Red Sea is Blue, Reports Spear-Shooting Zoologist; Woman Gets 300 Kinds of Poison Fish in Navy Study," *The New York Times*, November 6, 1951.

Ross, Michael. *Fish Watching with Eugenie Clark*. (Minneapolis: Carolrhoda Books, Inc., 2000).

"The Sharkman meets Eugenie Clark." (Sharkman's Graphics, www.sharkmans-world.com/eclark.html).

Stegman, Carolyn B. *Women of Achievement in Maryland History*. (Forest Park, MD: Anaconda Press, 2002, 229-230).

Washington, Lloyd Grove. "Shark-Riding U-Md. Scientist Gains Fans, Critics With Her Exploits," *The Washington Post,* December 8, 1981.

Chapter Notes

1. Clark, Eugenie. *Lady With a Spear*. (New York: Harper & Brothers, 1953).
2. Krueger, Curtis. "Curiosity Drover Her to Become 'Shark Lady,'" *St. Petersburg Times Online*, March 18, 2006. (www.sptimes.com/2006/03/18/Tampabay/Curiosity_drove_her_t.shtml).
3. Clark, Eugenie. *Lady With a Spear*. (New York: Harper & Brothers, 1953).
4. Krueger, Curtis. "Curiosity Drover Her to Become 'Shark Lady,'" *St. Petersburg Times Online*, March 18, 2006. (www.sptimes.com/2006/03/18/Tampabay/Curiosity_drove_her_t.shtml).

Lucille Clifton

Holladay, Hilary. *Wild Blessings, the Poetry of Lucille Clifton*. (Baton Rouge, LA: Louisiana State University Press, 2004).

Lupton, Mary Jane. *Lucille Clifton, Her Life and Letters*. (Westport, CT: Praeger, 2006).

Moody, Jocelyn K. "About Lucille Clifton," *Modern American Poetry*, compiled by Cary Nelson. (www.english.uiuc.edu/maps/poets/a_f/clifton/clifton.htm).

Collections of Poems by Lucille Clifton

An Ordinary Woman. (New York: Random House, 1974).

Blessing the Boats: New and Selected Poems, 1988-2000. (Rochester, NY: BOA Editions, 2000).

The Book of Light. (Port Townsend, WA: Copper Canyon, 1993).

Good Times: Poems. (New York: Random House, 1969).

Good News About the Earth: New Poems. (New York: Random House, 1972).

Good Woman: Poems and a Memoir, 1969-1980. (Brockport, NY: BOA Editions, 1987).

Next: New Poems. (Brockport, NY: BOA Editions, 1987).

Quilting: Poems, 1987-1990. (Brockport, NY: BOA Editions, 1991).

The Terrible Stories. (Brockport, NY: BOA Editions, 1996).

Two-Headed Woman. (Amherst, MA: University of Massachusetts Press, 1980).

Children's Books by Lucille Clifton

Amifika. (New York: Dutton, 1977).

The Black BC's. (New York: Dutton, 1970).

The Boy Who Didn't Believe in Spring. (New York: Dutton, 1973).

Don't You Remember? (New York: Dutton, 1973).

Everett Anderson's Christmas Coming. (New York: Holt, Rinehart and Winston, 1971).

Everett Anderson's Friend. (New York: Holt, Rinehart and Winston, 1976).

Everett Anderson's Goodbye. (New York: Holt, Rinehart and Winston, 1983).

Everett Anderson's 1,2,3. (New York: Holt, Rinehart and Winston, 1977).

Everett Anderson's Year. (New York: Holt, Rinehart and Winston, 1974).

Good, Says Jerome. (New York: Dutton, 1973).

The Lucky Stone. (New York: Delacorte Press, 1979).

My Brother Fine with Me. (New York: Holt, Rinehart and Winston, 1976).

One of the Problems of Everett Anderson. (New York: Holt, Rinehart and Winston, 2001).

Some of the Days of Everett Anderson. (New York: Holt, Rinehart and Winston, 1969).

Three Wishes. (New York: Viking Press, 1976).

The Times They Used to Be. (New York: Holt, Rinehart and Winston, 1974).

Cone Sisters

Carter, Ashley. "Inside the Cone Collection: Baltimore Sisters Amassed a Treasure Trove of Art," Naples Museum of Art. http://frugalfun.com/cone-collection.html

The Cone Collection: The Baltimore Museum of Art.

Cone, Edward. "Shirtsleeves to Matisses," *Forbes Magazine*, 1999. (www.forbes.com/forbes/1999/1011/6409098a_print.html)

"Cone Sisters," Teaching American History in Maryland. (Maryland State Archives, http://teachingamericanhistorymd.net).

DeVree, Charlotte. "Two Victorians in Modern Art," *The New York Times*, January 16, 1955.

"Etta Cone 1870-1949," *Dictionary of American Biography, Supplement 4: 1946-1950.* (American Council of Learned Societies, 1974).

Gabriel, Mary. *The Art of Acquiring: A Portrait of Etta and Claribel Cone.* (Baltimore, MD: Bancroft Press, 2002).

Holland, Cotter. "Sister Collectors, Ahead of Their Time," *The New York Times*, April 20, 2001.

Louchheim, Aline B. "Cone Bequest Enriches Baltimore," *The New York Times*. October 9, 1949.

Parke-Taylor, Michael. "Collecting Matisse: The Cone Sisters from Baltimore." (The Baltimore Museum of Art, www.ago.net/matisse-from-the-baltimore-museum-of-art).

Richardson, Brenda, *Dr. Claribel and Miss Etta.* (The Cone Collection of The Baltimore Museum of Art, 1985).

Russell, John. "Art View; Two Slow Starters Who Ended in Glory," *The New York Times*, November 10, 1985.

Selby, Holly. "A Family Affair: Relatives of the Cone Sisters Tour the New BMA Wing that Houses their Aunts' Collection," *The Baltimore Sun*, April 18, 2001.

Selby, Holly. "A Tale of Two Collectors," *The Baltimore Sun*, April 22, 2001.

"Selections from the Cone Wing," *The Baltimore Sun*, April 22, 2001.

"Virtual Tour of Cone Sisters' Apartment." (The Baltimore Museum of Art, 2001, http://www.artbma.org/video/conevideo.html).

Chapter Notes

1. The Baltimore Museum of Art's The Cone Collection, as quoted in Mary Gabriel's book, *The Art of Acquiring: A Portrait of Etta and Claribel Cone.* (Baltimore, MD: Bancroft Press, 2002, 87)
2. The Baltimore Museum of Art's The Cone Collection, as quoted in Mary Gabriel's book, *The Art of Acquiring: A Portrait of Etta and Claribel Cone.* (Baltimore, MD: Bancroft Press, 2002, 158)
3. *The Baltimore Sun*, April 15, 1928, as quoted in Mary Gabriel's book, *The Art of Acquiring: A Portrait of Etta and Claribel Cone.* (Baltimore, MD: Bancroft Press, 2002, 135)

Virginia Hall

Catling, Lorna. Phone Interview, February 20, 2008.
Haines, Gerald K. "Virginia Hall Goillot, Career Intelligence Officer." *Quarterly of the National Archives*, Winter 1994.
Nuckolls, Ben. *Ambassadors to Honor Female Spy*, ABC News, December 10, 2006.
Pearson, Judith. *The Wolves at the Door.* (Guilford, CT: The Globe Pequot Press, 2005).
Quid Nunc. Roland Park Country School Yearbook, 1924.
Schoettler, Carl. "Agent's Secrets," *The Baltimore Sun,* April 29, 2002.
Schoettler, Carl. "A Cloak-and-Dagger Life is Exposed for All to See," *The Baltimore Sun,* November 25, 2004.
Tucker, Abigail. "A Spy Gets Her Due," *The Baltimore Sun,* December 14, 2006.

Chapter Notes

1. Interview with Lorna Catling, February 20, 2008.
2. Ibid

Lillie Carroll Jackson

"Dr. Lillie M. Jackson Writes Her Own Story." *Baltimore Afro-American*, March 14, 1970.
Helmes, Winifred, G., ed., "Lillie May Jackson, 1889-1975 Civil Rights Activist," *Notable Maryland Women.* (Cambridge, MD: Tidewater Publishers, 1977).
"Lillie Carroll Jackson, Mother of a Movement," *The Baltimore Sun,* August 21,1999, 12A.
Oral History Interview, Virginia Jackson Mitchell and Juanita Jackson Mitchell interviewed by Charles Wagandt. (McKeldin-Jackson Oral History Collection, OH 8094, Maryland Historical Society, July 15, 1975).
Oral History Interview, Juanita Jackson Mitchell, interviewed by Charles Wagandt. (McKeldin-Jackson Oral History Collection, OH 8095, Maryland Historical Society, July 25, 1975).
Oral History Interview, Virginia Jackson Kiah, interviewed by Charles Wagandt. (McKeldin-Jackson Oral History Collection, OH 8097, Maryland Historical Society, January 10, 1976).
Oral History Interview, Louis Shub, interviewed by Ellen Paul. (McKeldin-Jackson Oral History Collection, OH 8100, Maryland Historical Society. 1976).

Oral History Interview, James Hepbron, interviewed by Barry Lanman. (McKeldin-Jackson Oral History Collection, OH 8152, Maryland Historical Society, July 21, 1976).

Oral History Interview, Raymond AC. Young, interviewed by Leroy Graham. (McKeldin-Jackson Oral History Collection, OH 8153, Maryland Historical Society, 1976).

Oral History Interview, Clarence M. Mitchell, Jr., interviewed by Leroy Graham. (McKeldin-Jackson Oral History Collection, OH 8154, Maryland Historical Society, July 29, 1976 and August 3, 1976).

Oral History Interview, Clarence M. Mitchell, Jr., interviewed by Charles Wagandt. (McKeldin-Jackson Oral History Collection, OH 8209, Maryland Historical Society, February 12, 1977).

Skotnes, Andor. Oral History Tapes and Notes. May 1995.

Smith, Jessie Carney, ed., *Notable Black American Women: Book II.* 758-759.

Stegman, Carolyn, B. *Women of Achievement in Maryland History.* (Forest Park, MD: Anaconda Press, 2002, 34).

Wagandt, Charles. "Lillie May and Teddy—They Led Baltimore Over and Around Race Relations." (Maryland Historical Society).

Chapter Notes

1. Interview with Juanita Jackson Mitchell. (McKeldin-Jackson Oral History Collection, OH 8095, Maryland Historical Society, July 25, 1975).
2. Interview with Virginia Jackson Mitchell and Juanita Jackson Mitchell. (McKeldin-Jackson Oral History Collection, OH 8094, Maryland Historical Society, July 15, 1975).
3. Interview with Juanita Jackson Mitchell. (McKeldin-Jackson Oral History Collection, OH 8095, Maryland Historical Society, July 25, 1975).

Claire McCardell

"The American Look," *Newsweek*, June 5, 1972.

"The American Look," *Time Magazine*, May 2, 1955. (www.time.com/time/magazine/article/0,9171,866314-1,00.html)

Apgar, Dorothy. "Changing Fashions Reflect Changing Views of Women," *The News American*, August 19, 1973.

Claire McCardell Collection, 1923-1995, MS 3066. (H. Furlong Baldwin Library, Maryland Historical Society).

"Claire McCardell and the American Look," *The Baltimore Sun*, August 7, 1999.

"Claire McCardell, Designer, Dies," *The New York Times*, March 23, 1958.

Ikenberg, Tamara. "Local Pioneers Parlayed Talent, Became Legends," *The Baltimore Sun*, January 30, 2000

Robb, Inez. "Claire McCardell Had the Right Idea," *The Camden Courier*, March 28, 1958.

Martin, Richard. *American Ingenuity: Sportswear, 1930s–1970s.* (The Costume Institute, The Metropolitan Museum of Art, www.metmuseum.org/toah/hd/amsp/hd_amsp.htm)

McCardell, Claire. "What Shall I Wear?" *McCall's Condensed Book*, November 1956.

Stegman, Carolyn B. *Women of Achievement in Maryland History.* (University Park, MD: Women of Achievement in Maryland History, 2002, 275-276).

Yohannan, Kohle. *Claire McCardell: Redefining Modernism.* (New York: Harry N. Abrams, 1998).

Stucker, Jan Collins and Jane Gerhard. "McCardell, Claire (1905-1958)," *American Decades*, Online ed., Ed. Tandy McDonnell. (Detroit: Gale, 2003).

Chapter Notes

1. Letter dated August 27, 1926, to her parents. Claire McCardell Collection, 1923-1995, MS 3066. H. Furlong Baldwin Library, Maryland Historical Society. Box 1
2. Letter dated August 28, 1926, to her parents. Claire McCardell Collection, 1923-1995, MS 3066. H. Furlong Baldwin Library, Maryland Historical Society. Box 1
3. Letter to her parents. No Date. Claire McCardell Collection, 1923-1995, MS 3066. H. Furlong Baldwin Library, Maryland Historical Society. Box 1
4. Letter to her parents. No Date. Claire McCardell Collection, 1923-1995, MS 3066. H. Furlong Baldwin Library, Maryland Historical Society. Box 1
5. Letter to her parents. No Date.Claire McCardell Collection, 1923-1995, MS 3066. H. Furlong Baldwin Library, Maryland Historical Society. Box 1

Barbara Mikulski

Abalyan, Karine, "Senate's 'Sweet 16' Calls Mikulski No. 1." *The Monitor*. (McAllen, TX: December 5, 2006).

"Barbara Mikulski," (Gale Biography Resource Center).

"Barbara A. Mikulski," NASW Foundation National Programs, 1997. (www.socialworkersfoundation.org).

Barbara Mikulski. Answers.com. (www.answers.com/topic/barbara-mikulski).

"Barbara Mikulski United States Senator—Maryland,"*PolishNews*, 2002. (www.polishnews.com).

Mikulski, Barbara. Online Interview, June 2007.

Mikulski, Barbara. "Who Speaks for Ethnic America?" *The New York Times*, September 29, 1970, 43.

Nine and Counting: The Women of the Senate. Written with Catherine Whitney. (New York: William Morrow, 2000).

Pollack, Jill W. *Women of the Hill: A History of Women in Congress*. (New York: Franklin Watts, 1996, 152-157).

Presa, Rachel. "Bigwigs Drop Big Bucks into the Bay," *Bay Weekly*, 2001. (www.bayweekly.com)

"US Senator, DC. Barbara Mikulski." Maryland Democratic Party. (www.mddems.org).

Chapter Notes

1. Interview with Barbara Mikulski, June 2007.
2. Ibid
3. Ibid
4. Ibid

Sadie Kneller Miller

"A Baltimore Woman's Success with a Camera," *The Baltimore Sun*, October 20, 2007.

Helmes, Winifred, G. *Notable Maryland Women*. (Cambridge, MD: Tidewater Publishers, 234-237).

Interview. *Baltimore American*, October 20, 1907.

Miller, Sadie Kneller. "Women's Trip Through Baltimore New Sewer in an Automobile." *Leslie's Weekly*, September 16, 1909.

Mitchell, Helen Buss. "S.K.Miller, A Double Exposure," *Extra, News American*, February 10, 1974.

"On the Staff of Leslie's Weekly," *Western Maryland Alumni Bulletin,* Vol. 1, No. 1, March 1914.

Richwine, Keith. "Mrs. Miller's Maryland," Western Maryland College, The Maryland Committee for the Humanities, February 22, 1983.

Ross, Isabel. *Ladies of the Press.* (New York: Harper & Brothers, 1936. 47-48).

Sadie Kneller Miller. Maryland Women's Hall of Fame. (www.msa.md.gov/msa/educ/ exhibits/womenshall/html/miller.html)

Scott, Dean."The Story of a Pioneer Lady Journalist," *County Wide Newspaper*, March 23, 1988.

"The Senators Slump," *The Washington Post* , August 12, 1985.

Sheridan, George. "The World's Only Woman Correspondent," *Leslie's Weekly*, February 27, 1913.

Stegman, Carolyn B. *Women of Achievement in Maryland History.* (Forest Park, MD: Anaconda Press, 2002, 322).

Chapter Notes

1. Sheridan, George. "The World's Only Woman Correspondent," *Leslie's Weekly*, February 27, 1913.
2. Mitchell, Helen Buss. "S.K.Miller, A Double Exposure," *Extra, News American*, February 10, 1974.
3. *Leslie's Weekly*, Feb. 27, 1913.
4. *Extra, News American*, February, 10, 1974.
5. Richwine, Keith. "Mrs. Miller's Maryland," Western Maryland College, The Maryland Committee for the Humanities, February 22, 1983.

Alta Schrock

Baldwin, Fred. *Appalachia: Journal of the Appalachian Regional Commission,* Vol. 27, # 4, Fall 1994.

Reppert, Ralph. "Encouraging Mountain Crafts and Talents," *The Sunday Sun Magazine.* September 29, 1963.

Schrock, Ada. "Mover of Mountains," *The Casselman Valley Chronicles.* (Springs, PA: Springs Historical Society of the Casselman Valley, Volume XVIII, numbers 3 and 4, 1978).

Schrock, Ada. Personal Interview. July 24, 2007.

Schrock, Alta. "Annie Rooney—A Tribute," *The Casselman Valley Chronicles.* (Springs, PA: Springs Historical Society of the Casselman Valley, Volume XVIII, numbers 3 and 4, 1978).

Schrock, Alta. "Graduate School During the Great Depression," *The Casselman Valley Chronicles.* (Springs, PA: Springs Historical Society of the Casselman Valley, Volume XXXIX, number 2, 1999).

Schrock, Alta. "More About Ethel," *The Casselman Valley Chronicles.* (Springs, PA: Springs Historical Society of the Casselman Valley, Volume XXXIX, number 2,1999).

Schrock, Alta. "Nature's Alarm Clocks," *The Casselman Valley Chronicles.* (Springs, PA: Springs Historical Society of the Casselman Valley, Volume XXXIX, number 2,1999).

Schrock, Alta. "The Schrocks of Strawberry Hill," *The Casselman Valley Chronicles.* (Springs, PA: Springs Historical Society of the Casselman Valley, Volume 2, 1999).

Wiley, Phoebe A. E-mail to Frostburg State University faculty and staff, November 8, 2001.

Helen Taussig

Altman, Lawrence K. "Dr. Helen Taussig, 87, Dies," *The New York Times,* May 22, 1986.

Anne T. Keene. "Taussig, Helen Brooke,"*American National Biography*. (www.anb.org/articles/12/12-01892.html)

Baldwin, Joyce. *To Heal the Heart of a Child.* (New York, NY: Walker and Company, 1992).

"Dr. Helen Brooke Taussig," *Changing the Face of Medicine.* (www.nlm.nih.gov/changingthefaceofmedicine/physicians/biography_316.html)

Dibell, Kathie. "She'll Follow Up On Blue Babies," *The Washington Post,* December 23, 1964.

"Dr. Helen Taussig: Pioneer cardiologist," *The Baltimore Sun,* July 17, 1999, 8A.

"Helen Brooke Taussig," *Encyclopedia of World Biography*, Ed. Suzanne M. Bourgoin, 2nd ed. (Detroit, MI: Gale Research, 1998).

McLaren, Karen, "Helen Brooke Taussig." *Encyclopedia Britannica eb.com* (www.britannica.com/EBchecked/topic/584426/Helen-Taussig)

Zinkham, William H. M.D. Personal Interview, February 5, 2008.

Chapter Notes

1. Interview with Dr. William H. Zinkham, Feburary, 5, 2008.

Mary Lemist Titcomb

Booth, Charles E. "Miss Mary's Book Wagon," *American Mercury*, Volume LXXXVII, September 1958.

Brown, Eleanor F. *Bookmobiles and Bookmobile Service* (Metuchen, NY: The Scarecrow Press, 1967).

Smith, William, ed. *Antique Automobile,* May-June, 1994.

Titcomb, Mary L. and Mary Louise Holzapfel. *The Washington County Free Library, 1901-1951.* (Hagerstown, Maryland, 1951).

Wilkerson, Mary. *Pioneering Leaders in Librarianship.* (Chicago, IL: The American Library Association, 1953).

Wynar, Bohdan, ed. *Dictionary of American Library Biography.* (Littleton, CO: Libraries Unlimited, 1978).

Emily Hammond Wilson Walker

Furgurson, E.B. III. "More Than a Doctor: South County Pioneer Dies at 103," *Capital Gazette Newspaper.* (www.hometownannapolis.com/news/top/2007/07/11-37).

Magnotti, Therese. *Doc: The Life of Emily Hammond Wilson.* (Shady Side, MD: Shady Side Rural Heritage Society, Inc., 1995).

Rasmussen, Frederick N. "Emily W. Walker." *The Baltimore Sun,* July 14, 2007.

Sullivan, Patricia. "Emily Wilson Walker, 103," *The Washington Post,* July12, 2007.

Wilson, Christopher. Personal Interview. August 27, 2007.

Wilson, John. Personal Interview. August, 27, 2007.

Winters, Wendi. "Doc Emily Hammond Wilson: A Medical Pioneer in South County," *What's Up Annapolis?*, March 2006.

Chapter Notes

1. Magnotti, Therese. *Doc: The Life of Emily Hammond Wilson*. (Shady Side, MD: Shady Side Rural Heritage Society, Inc., 1995, 27).
2. Ibid, 31
3. Ibid, 39
4. Ibid, 42

Verda Welcome

"An Issue That Mixes Politics and Race," *The Baltimore Sun*, February 17, 1991, 1E.

Oral History Interview, Verda Welcome, interviewed by Ellen Paul. (McKeldin-Jackson Oral History Collection, OH 8145, Maryland Historical Society, July 8, 1976).

Stegman, Carolyn B. *Women of Achievement in Maryland History*. (Forest Park, MD: Anaconda Press, 2002, 390-391).

Thompson, Garland, L. "Welcome's 'Life and Times' Full of Lessons About Civil Rights," *The Baltimore Sun*, March 15, 1992, 8C.

"Verda Freeman Welcome," *Notable Black American Women, Book 2*. (Farmington Hills, MI: Gale Research, 1996. [Reproduced in Biography Resource Center, Thomson Gale, 2007]).

"Verda F. Welcome, 83, A Maryland Legislator," *The New York Times*, April 25, 1990.

Welcome, Verda F. as told to Abraham, James M. *My Life and Times*. (Englewood Cliffs, NJ: Henry House Publishers, 1991).

Chapter Notes

1. Interview with Verda Welcome. (McKeldin-Jackson Oral History Collection, OH 8145, Maryland Historical Society, July 8, 1976).
2. Welcome, Verda F. as told to Abraham, James M. *My Life and Times*. (Englewood Cliffs, NJ: Henry House Publishers, 1991).

Debbie Yow

Heller, Dick. "Wolfpack's Yow Hanging Tough," *The Washington Times*, January 30, 2007.

Hildebrand, Jennifer. "Yow: Reach for Dreams." *The Pendulum Online*, Elon University, April 18, 2002.

Kramer, Staci. "One to Watch," *The Sporting News*, September 5, 1994.

Yow, Debbie. Personal Interview. August 16, 2007.

Chapter Notes

1. Interview with Debbie Yow, August 16, 2007.
2. Ibid
3. Ibid
4. Ibid

Photography Credits

Page 8, Courtesy of Mary Bahr.

Page 11, Courtesy of Mary S. Bahr

Page 14, Courtesy of Helen Delich Bentley.

Page 27, Courtesy of Eugenie Clark and the Mote Marine Laboratory.

Page 36, Dr. Claribel Cone and Miss Etta Cone Papers, The Baltimore Museum of Art.

Page 42, The Central Intelligence Agency.

Page 54, Courtesy of Robert C. McCardell.

Page 60, Courtesy of Barbara Mikulski.

Page 65, Courtesy of *Leslie's Illustrated Weekly* and McDaniel College.

Page 70, Courtesy of Ann Hawthorne.

Page 81, Courtesy of The Western Maryland Historical Society.

Page 86, Courtesy of John and Christopher Wilson.

Page 93, Courtesy of Morgan State University.

Page 98, Courtesy of the University of Maryland, College Park.